PROBATE
Procedure Notes

KEVIN DONNELLY
Chief Clerk,
Winchester District Probate Registry

WATERLOW PUBLISHERS

First edition 1988
© Kevin Donnelly 1988

Waterlow Publishers
Oyez House, PO Box 55
27 Crimscott Street
London SE1 5TS
A division of Pergamon Financial and Professional Services PLC

ISBN 0 08 036898 0

British Library Cataloguing in Publication Data

Donnelly, Kevin
    Probate procedure notes.——(Procedure notes
series).
    1. England. Probate. Law
    I. Title II. Series
    344.2065'2

Printed in Great Britain by
A. Wheaton & Son Ltd, Exeter

Contents

Preface

References to "the Rules" or "r." are to the Non-Contentious Probate Rules 1987 unless otherwise indicated. The term "Registrar" denotes a Registrar of the Principal Registry or a district probate registrar unless the context suggests otherwise.

Any correspondence to the Principal Registry should be sent to the Receiver of Papers (if it is a covering letter with an application for a grant or resealing), to the Record Keeper (if the letter is a request for copies of a grant or for the amendment or revocation of a grant) or to the Chief Clerk of the Probate Department (if it is on any other aspect of probate) at the address given in section 1.4.3 below.

Correspondence to a district probate registry may be addressed to the District Probate Registrar or to the Chief Clerk. As from 1 August 1988 the central index and the index of caveats have been situated at the Leeds District Probate Registry.

The law is stated at 31 August 1988.

Table of Statutes

Table of Statutory Instruments and Directions

Table of Cases

1. Introduction

Contents

1.1   Introduction

1.1.1   The layout of this book is designed to enable the practitioner to
         apply for a grant in the estate of a deceased person on a step-by-step
         basis.

1.1.2   The chapters are arranged to coincide as nearly as possible with
         those in the 23rd edition of the *Probate Manual* (Waterlow, 1988)
         and there are references in the following chapters to various parts of
         that book.

1.1.3   The references to the *Probate Manual* are made mainly to enable the
         practitioner to find out further details on a particular subject outside
         the scope of this book, the purpose of which is to provide guidance
         in the basic type of application.

1.1.4   It should be possible to make an application armed with the will (if
         any), the correct form of oath and this book.

1.1.5   The following sections of this chapter set out the places in this book
         where details of a particular type of application will be found and the
         addresses where the applications can be made.

1.2   Types of application

1.2.1   There are four basic types of application for a grant of representation
         (or the equivalent):
         (a) Probate of the will
         (b) Letters of administration (with will)
         (c) Letters of administration
         (d) Reseals

1.2.2   Details in respect of applications for probate of the will of a person
         who died domiciled in England and Wales are set out in Chapter 3
         and Chapter 9 (trust corporations).

1.2.3   Applications for probate of the will are usually quite straightforward
         and there is therefore less reference in this book to this type of case.
         However, Chapter 7 section 7.5.2 (d) (foreign domicile) should be
         consulted in the event that the deceased died domiciled out of
         England and Wales leaving a will in English or Welsh.

1.2.4   Applications for letters of administration (with will) in the estates of
         persons who died domiciled in England and Wales are dealt with in
         Chapter 4. Further references will be found in Chapters 8 (minority
         interests and attorney grants), 9 (trust corporations), 10 (miscel-
         laneous grants) and 11 (*commorientes*). Foreign domicile applications
         for letters of administration (with will) are dealt with in Chapter 7.

1.2.5   Applications for letters of administration in the estates of persons
         who died domiciled in England and Wales are dealt with in Chapter
         5. Reference should also be made to the other chapters set out in
         section 1.2.4 above.

1.2.6   Reseals are dealt with in Chapter 12.

1.2.7   Reference to the contents page of each chapter will enable the
         relevant section to be located. Whenever possible, cross-references
         have been included in the sections.

1.3   General provisions

1.3.1   Applications (a) to (c) in section 1.2.1 above require an oath in
         support.
         (r. 8(1))

1.3.2   The oath should be sworn or affirmed before a person authorised so to do.
(Secretary's Circular, 12 April 1967)

1.3.3   Some Notaries Public in certain circumstances are entitled to administer the oath in applications for grants of representation.
(Administration of Justice Act 1985 s. 65)

1.3.4   Justices of the Peace and Stipendiary Magistrates acting in their official capacity cannot administer the oath in applications for grants of representation.

1.3.5   A solicitor cannot administer the oath in proceedings in which he is acting or in which any partner of his firm is acting.
(Solicitors Act 1974 s. 81(2))

1.3.6   Oaths can be sworn out of England and Wales before anyone so entitled to do by the law of the place where the documents are sworn.

1.3.7   Evidence as to the entitlement to swear such oaths in respect of section 1.3.6. above may be required by the Registrar before the application can proceed.

1.3.8   If the deponent is serving in the armed forces abroad, it is possible for certain officers of his branch of the service to administer the oath.
(Emergency Laws (Miscellaneous Provisions) Act 1953 s. 10; Army Act 1955 s. 204; Air Force Act 1955 s. 204 (as amended by s. 19 Armed Forces Act 1981))

1.4   Where to make the grant application

1.4.1   Applications for grants of representation may be made at any of the registries or sub-registries in section 1.4.3 below.

1.4.2   There is no territorial jurisdiction in respect of making applications for grants governing at which registry or sub-registry the application may be made.

1.4.3   The addresses, telephone, and document exchange (DX) numbers of the registries and, where appropriate, sub-registries of the group are as follows:

Principal Registry of the Family
Division
Probate Department
Somerset House
Strand
London WC2R 1LP
Tel: (01) 936 7000 (Record Keeper)/
6983 (Probate Enquiries)
DX: 396 London Chancery Lane

Birmingham District Probate
Registry (Main Registry)
3rd Floor, Cavendish House
Waterloo Street
Birmingham B2 5PS
Tel: (021) 236 6263/4560

Stoke-on-Trent Sub-Registry
2nd Floor, Town Hall
Albion Street
Hanley
Stoke-on-Trent ST1 1QL
Tel: (0782) 23736

Brighton District Probate Registry
(Main Registry)
William Street
Brighton BN2 2LG
Tel: (0273) 684071
DX: 2734 Brighton 1

Maidstone Sub-Registry
The Law Courts
Barker Road
Maidstone ME18 8EW
Tel: (0622) 54966
DX: 4846 Maidstone

Bristol District Probate Registry
(Main Registry)
The Crescent Centre
Temple Back
Bristol BS1 6EP
Tel: (0272) 273915/24619

Bodmin Probate Sub-Registry
Market Street
Bodmin
Cornwall PL31 2JW
Tel: (0208) 72279

Exeter Probate Sub-Registry
Eastgate House
High Street
Exeter
Devon EX4 3JZ
Tel: (0392) 74515

Ipswich District Probate Registry
(Main Registry)
Level 3, Haven House
17 Lower Brook Street
Ipswich IP4 1DN
Tel: (0473) 53724
DX: 3279 Ipswich

Norwich Probate Sub-Registry
The Law Courts
Bishopgate
Norwich
Norfolk NR3 1UR
Tel: (0603) 761776
DX: 5202 Norwich

Peterborough Probate Sub-Registry
Clifton House
Broadway
Peterborough PE1 1SL
Tel: (0733) 62802
DX: 12327 Peterborough 1

Leeds District Probate Registry
(Main Registry)
3rd Floor
Coronet House
Queen Street
Leeds LS1 2BA
Tel: (0532) 431505
DX: 26451 Leeds Park Square

Lincoln Probate Sub-Registry
Mill House
Brayford Side North
Lincoln LN1 1YW
Tel: (0522) 23648
DX: 17701 Lincoln 2

Sheffield Probate Sub-Registry
The Court House
Castle Street
Sheffield S3 8LW
Tel: (0742) 729920
DX: 26054 Sheffield 2

Liverpool District Probate Registry
(Main Registry)
3rd Floor, India Buildings
Water Street
Liverpool L2 0QR
Tel: (051) 236 8264

Chester Probate Sub-Registry
5th Floor, Hamilton House
Hamilton Place
Chester CH1 2DA
Tel: (0244) 45082

Lancaster Probate Sub-Registry
Mitre House
Church Street
Lancaster LA1 1HE
Tel: (0524) 36625

The Probate Registry of Wales
(Main Registry)
49 Cardiff Road
Llandaff
Cardiff CF5 2YW
Tel: (0222) 562422

Bangor Probate Sub-Registry
1st Floor, Bron Castell
High Street
Bangor LL57 1YS
Tel: (0248) 362410

Carmarthen Probate Sub-Registry
14 King Street
Carmarthen
Dyfed SA31 1BL
Tel: (0267) 236238

Gloucester Probate Sub-Registry
3 Pitt Street
Gloucester GL1 2BJ
Tel: (0452) 22585

Manchester District Probate Registry
(Main Registry)
9th Floor, Astley House
23 Quay Street
Manchester M3 4AT
Tel: (061) 834 4319
DX: 14387 Manchester

Nottingham Probate Sub-Registry
Upper Ground Floor
Lambert House
Talbot Street
Nottingham NG1 5NS
Tel: (0602) 414288
DX: 10055 Nottingham

Newcastle-upon-Tyne District
Probate Registry
(Main Registry)
2nd Floor, Plummer House
Croft Street
Newcastle-upon-Tyne NE1 6ND
Tel: (091) 261 8383
DX: 61081 Newcastle-upon-Tyne

Carlisle Probate Sub-Registry
2 Victoria Place
Carlisle CA1 1ER
Tel: (0228) 21751
DX 63034 Carlisle

Middlesbrough Probate Sub-Registry
12/16 Woodlands Road
Middlesbrough TS1 3BE
Tel: (0642) 244770

York Probate Sub-Registry
Duncome Place
York YO1 2EA
Tel: (0904) 624210
DX 61543 York

Leicester Probate Sub-Registry
Government Buildings
Newarke Street
Leicester LE1 5SE
Tel: (0533) 546117
DX: 10870 Leicester

Oxford District Probate Registry
(Main Registry)
10a New Road
Oxford OX1 1LY
Tel: (0865) 241163
DX: 4337 Oxford

Winchester District Probate Registry
(Main Registry)
4th Floor, Cromwell House
Andover Road
Winchester
Hampshire SO23 7EW
Tel: (0962) 53046/63771
DX: 2528 Winchester

1.5   Other addresses

1.5.1   It is sometimes necessary to contact other offices when making an application for a grant of representation.

1.5.2   Set out below are the addresses of other branches of the Supreme Court and Inland Revenue with whom it may be necessary to have dealings:

1.5.3   Capital Taxes Office: England and Wales

(a) General enquiries   – Capital Taxes Office
                           Minford House
                           Rockley Road
                           London W14 0DF
                           Tel: 01-603 4622

(b) Payment of tax   – Inland Revenue Finance Division
                           Barrington Road
                           Worthing
                           West Sussex BN12 4SF
                           Tel: (0903) 502525

(c) Control of accounts – Capital Taxes Office
                           Minford House
                           Rockley Road
                           London W14 0DF
                           Tel: 01-603 4622

1.5.4   Capital Taxes Office: Scotland

> Capital Taxes Office
> 16 Picardy Place
> Edinburgh EH1 3NB
> Tel: 031-556 8511

1.5.5   Capital Taxes Office: Northern Ireland

> Capital Taxes Office
> Law Court Buildings
> Chichester Street
> Belfast BT1 3NU
> Tel: (0232) 235111

1.5.6   The Treasury Solicitor:

> The Treasury Solicitor (B.V.)
> Queen Anne's Chambers
> 28 Broadway
> London SW1H 9JS
> Tel: 01-210 3117

1.5.7   Court of Protection:

> The Court of Protection
> 25 Store Street
> London WC1E 7BP
> Tel: 01-636 6877

1.5.8   Public Trustee:

> The Public Trustee Office
> Stewart House
> Kingsway
> London WC2B 6JX
> Tel: 01-405 4300

1.5.9   Grants of Representation – Scotland

> (a) Sheriff Clerk (Commissary Office)
>   16 North Bank Street
>   Edinburgh EH1 2NS
>   Tel: 031-226 7181
>
> (b) Sheriff Clerk of Glasgow and
>   Strathkelvin
>   County Buildings
>   149 Ingram Street
>   Glasgow G1 1SY

1.5.10   Grants of Representation – Northern Ireland

The Master
Probate and Matrimonial Office
Royal Courts of Justice (Ulster)
Chichester Street
Belfast BT1 3JE

2. Wills and Codicils

Contents

2.1   Validity of wills – introduction

2.1.1   Before making any application you must ascertain that the will you have to prove is valid. The following points relate solely to wills of persons who were domiciled in England and Wales both at the date of the will and at the date of death and to which no other form of internal law save that of England and Wales applied.

2.1.2   To be formally valid a will should:
(1) be in writing (Wills Act 1837 s. 9):
(2) be signed by or at the direction of the testator (Wills Act 1837 s. 9(a)). The signature can be by way of a mark or initials. The testator can acknowledge a previously made signature (Wills Act 1837 s. 9(c)):
(3) be signed or acknowledged by the testator as described above, in the presence of two witnesses who should then sign or, in the case of a date of death on or after 1 January 1983, sign or acknowledge their signatures in the testator's presence (Wills Act 1837 s. 9(c), (d)).

2.1.3   The signature of the testator can be on any part of the will and gives effect to the will when signed (Wills Act 1837 s. 9(b)). Affidavit evidence from one of the witnesses to confirm due execution may be

necessary if the position of the testator's signature gives rise to doubt as to good execution.
(r. 12(1))

2.1.4   No form of attestation is necessary on a will (Wills Act 1837 s. 9). However, evidence as to due execution will be required if there is no attestation clause confirming good execution (r. 12(1) and (2)). Evidence may be dispensed with in certain circumstances at the Registrar's discretion (r. 12(3)). If the testator is blind or illiterate or the will was signed by another person at the direction of the testator, the Registrar may require evidence that the testator had knowledge of the contents of the will (r. 13). This also applies if the testator's signature is shaky or illegible.

2.1.5   The will should bear a date on its face but a date on the endorsement may be sufficient. Absence of a date or a significant difference in the dates on the face and endorsement or two differing dates on the face of the will may require evidence to establish the date.
(r. 14(4))

2.1.6   Any alteration in the will not authenticated as set out in s. 21 of the Wills Act 1837 requires evidence to establish whether the alteration was made before execution unless it appears to the Registrar that the alterations are of no practical importance.
(r. 14(2))

2.1.7   Any attempt at burning, tearing or otherwise destroying a will may give rise to a presumption of revocation and evidence may be called for to rebut that presumption.
(r. 15)

2.2   Form of the will

2.2.1   The form of the will should also be considered before applying for the grant.

2.2.2   Words can be omitted by way of a Registrar's order either:
(1) by reason of their nature (i.e. if the words are offensive, libellous or blasphemous)
(2) by way of an order under s. 20 of the Administration of Justice Act 1982 (r. 55). Words can also be added to a will under this section (see section 14.1 below).

2.2.3   A Registrar can also direct that an engrossment of a will be filed if a copy of the original will is not satisfactory for record purposes. (r. 11(1)).

2.2.4   An engrossment is also required if an order for rectification has been made under s. 20(1) of the Administration of Justice Act 1982. (r. 11(2)) (see section 14.1 below)
    The engrossment should follow as closely as possible the form of the original will or the will as rectified. (r. 11(3))

2.2.5   Any document which may be fit for incorporation should be produced to the Registrar for his decision. (r. 14(3))

2.3   Codicils

2.3.1   A codicil is subject to the same tests as to validity, form and content as a will.

2.4   Revocation of the will

2.4.1   A will may be revoked by:
    (1) a later will expressly (or in some cases implicitly) revoking all earlier documents, by burning, tearing or destroying by the testator or by someone at his direction and in his presence (Wills Act 1837 s. 20), or
    (2) subsequent marriage (unless made in contemplation of marriage) (Wills Act 1837 s. 18(1)).

2.5   Revocation of codicils

2.5.1   A codicil may be revoked in the same manner *but* it is not possible to change its effect on the will by such revocation.

2.6   Privileged wills

2.6.1   Wills made by a member of H.M. Forces on actual military service are not subject to the same general rules of validity (Wills Act 1837 s. 11).

2.6.2   A privileged will need not be written, witnessed or even signed and will be held to be valid provided that the testator was on actual military service at the date it was made and that at that date he was domiciled in England and Wales.

2.6.3   An affidavit confirming the facts set out in section 2.6.2 above is required, together with, in the event that the will has been written down, an affidavit confirming the signature or handwriting on the will as that of the testator or, if not written, what was said.

2.6.4   If the Registrar is satisfied with the evidence, the will is admitted to proof in the usual way.

2.7   Documents which cannot be proved

2.7.1   A will which does not appoint an executor or attempt to dispose of any estate.

2.7.2   A will which simply revokes all previous testamentary documents.

2.7.3   A document which takes effect during the lifetime of the person who executes it or upon a contingency which does not occur.

2.7.4   A will which has been marked 'probate refused' by a Registrar. (r. 12(1))

2.8   Miscellaneous points

2.8.1   A will need not be one document.

2.8.2   A will may be conditional. Evidence will be required as to the fulfilment of the condition.

2.8.3   *Joint and mutual wills*. A joint will is made by two individuals separately disposing of their property. It is admissible to proof on the death of the first testator. A mutual will is one (or two) testamentary documents which give similar rights to each testator and *may* create a trust making full effective revocation by one of the parties difficult.

2.8.4   A will may exercise a power of appointment.

2.8.5   A nuncupative will (i.e. a will which is not written down) or a copy or reconstructed will may be proved after obtaining an order of the Registrar (r. 54). If it is wished to prove such a will evidence of the following is required:

(1) that the original will was in existence at the deceased's date of death;

(2) in respect of a reconstruction of a will, that the reconstruction is accurate;

(3) in respect of a nuncupative will, that the contents are accurate (r. 54(4)).

Further evidence may be called for at the direction of the Registrar (r. 54(4)).

(For forms of affidavits of execution and other affidavits connected with the validity of a will or its contents see the precedents at paragraph 2.151 of the *Probate Manual*, 23rd edition).

2.9   Foreign domicile

2.9.1   Applications to prove a will in England and Wales of all persons domiciled in or out of England and Wales who died on or after 1 January 1964 are subject to the Wills Act 1963.

2.9.2   Generally speaking to be valid, a will must be executed in accordance with the internal law of the place where it was executed or where, at the date of execution or of the testator's death, he was domiciled or habitually resident or in a state of which at either time he was a national (Wills Act 1963 s. 1). If none of these conditions apply, the will may still be valid under one of the other provisions of the Act (see paragraphs 2.101ff of the *Probate Manual*, 23rd edition).

2.9.3   It should be noted that special considerations apply in the case of a person domiciled out of England and Wales whose estate in England and Wales consists wholly or substantially of immovable property (see sections 7.5.23 to 7.5.26 below).

2.9.4   See Chapter 7 for further details of foreign domicile.

3. Applications for Probate

3.1 Introduction

3.1.1 An application for probate of the will is made by an executor named in the will, by an executor appointed by the will (e.g. "my wife" without naming her) or an executor according to the tenor of the will. This last consists of a will with no specified executor but which names a person or persons whose duties, as set out in the will, closely approximate the duties of an executor (*re Brown's Goods* (1910) 54 Sol. Jo. 478).

3.1.2 The following applies to estates of persons domiciled in England and Wales. See Chapter 7 for the practice in respect of executors of deceased persons who died domiciled out of England and Wales.

3.1.3 The executor has to swear an oath in support of his application (or make a suitable affirmation).

3.1.4 The oath should contain:
   (a) details applicable to the estate (r. 8(1))
   (b) the deceased's domicile, unless the Registrar otherwise directs (r. 8(2))
   (c) on dates of death after 1 January 1926, a statement to the best of the executor's knowledge, information and belief as to whether or not the deceased died possessed of settled land (r. 8(3))
   (d) in the event that it is necessary, clearing to deal with an executor who is by the happening of a contingency no longer entitled to apply for a grant of probate and who had on the face of the will a prior title to a grant to that of the applicant.
(For forms of oath, see the precedents at paragraph 3.27 of the *Probate Manual*, 23rd edition).

3.2 Special practice points to consider in the oath

3.2.1 If the name of the executor is given incorrectly in the will, the true name and the name in the will should be shown on the oath and the identity of the executor accounted for to the satisfaction of the Registrar.

3.2.2 The order of executors should follow that set out in the will. If it is desired to have the grant issue with a differing order, the consents of all the proving executors should be lodged with the application.

3.2.3 The documents to be proved (i.e. the will and codicils, if any), are identified in the oath and should be marked with the signatures of the deponents and the person before whom the oath is sworn. (r. 10(1)(a))

3.2.4 The original will and codicils (if any) should be marked as in section 3.2.3 above unless:
   (1) the Registrar gives leave for a copy to be so marked (r. 10(2))
   (2) the original will or codicil is not available owing to it having been retained by a foreign court or official, in which case a properly certified copy issued by the court or official can be admitted to proof without the need for an order under r. 54(1) and marked accordingly
   (3) the Registrar has made an order admitting a copy or reconstructed will to proof (r. 54(1)), in which case the copy or reconstruction is marked.

3.2.5 If the grant is to issue including a name other than the deceased's true name, the executor should swear as to the true name and give reasons for the inclusion of the alias (e.g. the will has been made in another name or there are assets held in another name). (r. 9)

3.2.6 Up to three former addresses for the deceased can be included in the oath, provided that there is a specific reason for their inclusion and the total number of addresses given for the deceased does not exceed four.

3.2.7 If the exact date of death cannot be sworn, death should be sworn to have occurred between two dates as close together as possible (e.g. "last seen (or last known to be) alive on the . . . , dead body found on the . . .").

3.2.8   If the age cannot be sworn with certainty, the approximate age should be shown and the fact indicated in the oath.

3.2.9   All the executors appointed by the will can make the initial application for probate, up to a maximum of four (Supreme Court Act 1981 s. 114(1)).

3.2.10   The description of the executor in the oath is governed by the number and sex of the executors appointed: one male – sole executor, one female – sole executrix, one male and one female – the executors, two females – the executrixes, etc.

3.2.11   An executor who is not a specifically named person requires more detailed attention when making the application.

3.2.12   An appointment of a firm is held to be of all the partners in that firm *at the date of the will* unless there is anything in the text of the will to indicate otherwise (*re Fernie* (1849) 6 Notes of Cases 657). The appointment should be of the firm or of all the partners of the firm. Any other wording (e.g. two of the partners, any of the partners) is *prima facie* void (*re Bayliss's Goods* (1862) Swabey & Tristram's Reports 613, *re Blackwell's Goods* (1877) LR P & M 72). Such appointments can be saved by way of evidence under s. 21 of the Administration of Justice Act 1982 or, in suitable circumstances and more rarely, s. 20 of that Act.

3.2.13   An appointment of the holder of an office is deemed to be the holder of the office *at the date of death of the deceased* unless the will indicates otherwise (*re Jones* (1927) 43 TLR 324).

3.2.14   A trust corporation is defined in r. 1(2). A corporation (other than a trust corporation) does *not* have the right to take a grant of probate (r. 36(4)(a)). See Chapter 9 for further details in respect of corporations.

3.2.15   Any one of the executors appointed in the will can take a grant of probate (save for non-trust corporations) but all the other executors must be accounted for on the oath.

3.2.16   If an executor is no longer alive at the time of the first application for the grant, the other executors are described as "surviving executors".

3.2.17   The renunciation of any executor should be recited on the oath. The form of renunciation must be lodged with the papers in support of the application. (See Chapter 16 for further details of renunciations.)

3.2.18 (1) If the non-proving executors are to have power reserved for the making of a like grant in the future, this must be recited in the margin or in the body of the oath.

(2) Notice should be given to all executors to whom power is reserved (r. 27(1)), unless the Registrar agrees to dispense with the giving of such notice on the grounds that it is impracticable so to do or that unreasonable delay or expense would result if notice were to be given (r. 27(3)).

(3) Notice to partners in a firm who have been appointed executor may be given by sending it to its principal or last known place of business (r. 27(2)).

(4) Notice may be given in respect of (3) above in accordance with Order 65 r. 5 of the Rules of the Supreme Court 1965 (r. 67).

3.2.19 The oath should contain the gross and net figures of the estate or the 'band' figures in an excepted estate appropriate to the date of death, in accordance with the Capital Transfer Tax (Delivery of Accounts) Regulations 1981 (as amended). If the estate is an excepted estate, the oath should contain a statement that an Inland Revenue account is not required to be delivered. (For further details on excepted estates, see section 6.3 below.)

3.3 Double probate

3.3.1 If it is wished to extract a further grant of probate, this is done by one or more of the executors to whom power has been reserved on the original grant. This is known as a grant of double probate.

(For further details see paragraphs 3.28ff of the *Probate Manual*, 23rd edition.)

3.4 Miscellaneous points

3.4.1 Only an executor can apply for a grant of probate. A "mixed grant" of probate and letters of administration (with will) cannot be issued, even if it is the attorney of an executor who wishes to join in the application.

3.4.2 Where a sole executor is by reason of mental incapacity incapable of managing his affairs, a grant of letters of administration (with will) for his use and benefit until further representation be granted may be issued to the person entitled thereto under r. 35. For further information on this point, see section 8.6. below.

3.4.3   If after making his will, the testator's marriage is dissolved or
        annulled, the will takes effect as if the appointment of the spouse as
        executor or trustee was omitted (Wills Act 1837 s. 18A(1)(a)). Any
        gift to the ex-spouse lapses unless the will expresses a contrary
        intention (Wills Act 1837 s. 18A(1)(b)).
            See *Re Sinclair* [1985] 1 All ER 1066, [1985] 2 WLR 795 CA
        for the interpretation of "lapse".
            It should be noted that this section applies to foreign decrees
        which are capable of recognition in England and Wales by virtue of
        Part II of the Family Law Act 1986.

3.4.4   An executor who proves his testator's will becomes the executor by
        way of chain of executorship of all the estates of which that testator
        was sole or last surviving, proving executor (Administration of
        Estates Act 1925 s. 7).

3.4.5   No grant of probate will issue within seven days of the death of the
        deceased unless leave is given by the Registrar for it to be issued
        within that period.
        (r. 6(2))

3.4.6   Occasionally, executors with limited powers will be appointed (e.g.
        for an estate in a particular country or for a literary estate). The oath
        should be worded accordingly and care should be taken in prep-
        aration of the papers to make sure that all the executors have been
        described accurately and have been accounted for.

4. Applications for Letters of Administration (with Will)

Contents

4.1 Letters of administration (with will) – introduction

4.1.1 A grant of letters of administration (with will) is made whenever a will is proved by someone other than the executor.

4.1.2 The order of priority of persons entitled to apply is set out in r. 20:
  (1) Residuary legatee and devisee in trust for any other person (r. 20(b)).
  (2) (a) Any other residuary legatee or devisee or, where the residue is not disposed of by the will, the person entitled to the undisposed of residue (r. 20(c)).
      (b) There is an exception to the above which is dealt with in section 4.5.6 below.
  (3) The personal representative of any residuary legatee or devisee (save of a residuary legatee or devisee for life or of one holding the residuary estate in trust for any other person) or of a person entitled to the undisposed of residue (r. 20(d)).
  (4) Any legatee or devisee or creditor (r. 20(e)).
  (5) The personal representative of any legatee or devisee (save of one for life or of one holding the bequest in trust for someone else or any creditor of the deceased (r. 20(f)).

4.2　Examples of terms used in r. 20

4.2.1　residuary legatee or devisee in trust – 20(b) – "all my estate to A_____ B_____ on trust".

4.2.2　(a)　residuary legatee – 20(c) – "all my personal estate".
(b)　residuary devisee – 20(c) – "all my real estate".
(c)　residuary legatee and devisee – 20(c) – "all the remainder of my estate".

4.2.3　(a)　specific legatee – 20(d) – "£200.00 to A_____ B_____".
(b)　specific devisee – 20(d) – "my freehold property to A_____ B_____".

4.2.4　specific beneficiary for life – 20(e) – "my freehold property at/my shares in Moth Preservatives Ltd to A_____ B_____ for her life and upon her death to C_____ D_____".

4.2.5　vested interest – 20(c)(i), (e) – "£200.00 to A_____ B_____ absolutely".

4.2.6　contingent interest – 20(c)(i), (e) – "£200.00 to A_____ B_____ if she shall attain the age of 21 years".

4.2.7　It should be noted that a legatee is the recipient of a gift of personal estate, a devisee of real estate.

4.3　Grant to residuary legatee or devisee in trust

4.3.1　A person or persons to whom the residuary estate is given "upon trust" has priority over all other persons (save an executor) to prove a will (r. 20(b)).

4.3.2　The executor must be accounted for on the oath (e.g. by renunciation or death) and should be cleared off by reciting the fact.

4.4　Grant to residuary legatee or devisee

4.4.1　Any other residuary legatee or devisee (including one for life) is, upon clearing executors and residuary legatees and devisees in trust, next entitled to take the grant (r. 20(c)).

4.4.2   As in section 4.3.2 above, all persons with a prior title to the grant must be accounted for in the oath.

4.4.3   A residuary beneficiary with a vested interest will be preferred to a residuary beneficiary with a contingent interest (r. 20(c) proviso (i)).

4.4.4   A residuary beneficiary entitled to the estate in the event of a contingency is entitled to a grant before the happening of the contingency as well as after its happening.

4.4.5   If a life or minority interest arises under the will, two applicants are required unless the Registrar otherwise directs or a trust corporation proves the will (Supreme Court Act 1981 s. 114(2)).

4.5   Grant to persons entitled to the undisposed of residue

4.5.1   Reasons for no disposition of residue:
(a) inadequate wording of the will, resulting in failure to make a residuary gift.
(b) the residuary beneficiary has predeceased the testator and there is no other residuary beneficiary. Exception to this is the gift to a child (or other issue) of the testator. In this case, the gift is saved and passes:
(i) to the person entitled to the *estate* of the deceased beneficiary if the testator died *before* 1 January 1983 (Wills Act 1837 s. 33)
(ii) to the *issue* of the deceased beneficiary living at the date of death of the testator if the testator died *on or after* 1 January 1983 (Administration of Justice Act 1982 s. 19).

4.5.2   It should be noted that a will may dispose of the residuary personal estate but leave the residuary real estate undisposed of (or vice-versa).

4.5.3   If there is no effective disposition of residue under the will, a grant can be made to the persons entitled to the estate not disposed of (r. 20(c)).

4.5.4   The persons so entitled are entitled to the grant in the order of priority set out in r. 22 (see section 5.2 below for further details).

4.5.5   The same provisions as to the surviving spouse's statutory legacy apply in respect of undisposed of estate and in the event of a life interest arising, two applicants are usually required (Supreme Court Act 1981 s. 114(2)).

4.5.6   The exception to sections 4.5.3 and 4.5.4 above is the case when *the whole or substantially the whole* of the estate is disposed of by the will without there being a residuary gift. In these circumstances, any legatee or devisee may apply for a grant. (r. 20(c)(ii))

4.5.7   In the event that there is no-one entitled to the undisposed of estate as set out in r. 22, the Treasury Solicitor may claim bona vacantia on behalf of the Crown and apply for a grant. (r. 20(c))

4.6   Grant to personal representative of residuary legatee or devisee

4.6.1   If there is no person entitled to apply for a grant in sections 4.3 to 4.5 above, the personal representative of a residuary legatee or devisee may apply for a grant. (r. 20(d))

4.6.2   The residuary beneficiary must have survived the deceased (unless 4.5.1 above also applies).

4.6.3   The right to apply for a grant does not include personal representatives of residuary beneficiaries who held the estate in trust or had only a life interest.

4.6.4   The same factors as set out in sections 4.6.1 and the first part of 4.6.2 above apply to the personal representative of a person entitled to share in the residue not disposed of by the will.

4.7   Grant to specific legatee or devisee

4.7.1   In the event that all persons entitled to a grant in sections 4.3 to 4.6 above can be cleared off, the grant may issue to any specific legatee or devisee or to any creditor. (r. 20(e))

4.7.2   A legatee or devisee whose interest is vested will be preferred to one whose interest is contingent unless the Registrar otherwise directs. (r. 20(e))

4.8 **Grant to the personal representative of a legatee or devisee or creditor**

4.8.1 In the event that all persons entitled to a grant in sections 4.3 to 4.7 above can be cleared off, the grant may issue to the personal representative of any legatee, devisee or creditor.
(r. 20(f))

4.8.2 The beneficiary must have survived the deceased (unless 4.5.1(b) above applies).

4.8.3 The right to apply for a grant does not include a personal representative of a beneficiary whose gift was for life or held in trust for anyone else.

4.9 **Special practice points to consider on the oath**

4.9.1 Sections 3.2.1 and 3.2.3 to 3.2.8 above all apply to the oath to be sworn in respect of an application for letters of administration (with will).

4.9.2 (a) It must be stated in the oath whether any minority or life interest arises (r. 8(4)).
(b) (i) If this cannot be sworn in terms, the words "may arise" should be used in respect of the interest about which there is doubt.
(ii) In these circumstances, two applicants will be required unless the Registrar otherwise directs or a trust corporation takes the grant (Supreme Court Act 1981 s. 114(2)).

4.9.3 The correct title of the applicant (as defined in sections 4.3 to 4.8 above) and the clearing appropriate to the case should both be set out in full. (See the precedents at paragraphs 4.45 to 4.47 of the *Probate Manual*, 23rd edition.)

4.10 **Miscellaneous points**

4.10.1 (a) If a life or minority interest arises (or may arise) under the will, two applicants are usually required (Supreme Court Act 1981 s. 114(2)).
(b) The second applicant should have an equal title with that of the first (e.g. two residuary legatees and devisees).
(c) If there is no-one with an equal title as in (b) above, the second applicant can be of the next class under r. 20 (e.g. a residuary legatee and the personal representative of a residuary devisee).

4.10.2   (a)   (i)   If a witness is also a beneficiary or the husband or wife of a beneficiary, the gift to that beneficiary is void (Wills Act 1837 s. 15).

           (ii)   The beneficiary cannot take a grant *by virtue of a title achieved by that gift* (r. 21).

      (b)   This does not apply to persons who are entitled to the undisposed of residue or to those entitled to a grant as creditor or under sections 4.6 and 4.8 above.

4.10.3   The wording which may constitute residue is a difficult area to define clearly. Generally speaking, words are interpreted in the context of the will. (*Perrin v Morgan* [1943] AC 399, [1943] All ER 187 House of Lords).

4.10.4   A maximum number of four applicants can take out a grant of letters of administration (with will) (Supreme Court Act 1981 s. 114(1)).

4.10.5   Residuary beneficiaries (other than those holding in trust) and persons entitled to the undisposed of residue have equal title to a grant of letters of administration (with will).
(r. 20(c))

4.10.6   (a)   An executor may renounce probate and take a grant in a lower capacity (e.g. as residuary legatee and devisee) (r. 37(1)).

      (b)   A person entitled to a grant of administration (with will) cannot renounce his right to a grant in one capacity and take a grant in a lower capacity unless the Registrar otherwise directs (e.g. as residuary legatee and devisee in trust, renounce letters of administration (with will) and take a grant as residuary legatee and devisee (r. 37(2)).

4.10.7   Persons with a higher title than that of the applicant must be cleared off in the oath and the appropriate renunciations lodged with the application.

4.10.8   Grants of letters of administration (with will) to trust corporations and to corporations other than trust corporations are dealt with in Chapter 9.

5. Applications for Letters of Administration

5.1   General principles

5.1.1 When a person dies without leaving a will (wholly intestate) a grant of letters of administration is issued.

5.2   Persons entitled to a grant

5.2.1 The order of priority of persons entitled to apply for a grant of letters of administration is set out in r. 22 and is as follows:

5.2.2 Surviving spouse.
     (r. 22(1)(a))

5.2.3   Children of the deceased or the issue of children who died before the deceased.
        (r. 22(1)(b))

5.2.4   Parents of the deceased.
        (r. 22(1)(c))

5.2.5   Brothers or sisters of the whole blood or the issue of brothers or sisters of the whole blood who died before the deceased.
        (r. 22(1)(d))

5.2.6   Brothers or sisters of the half blood or the issue of brothers or sisters of the half blood who died before the deceased.
        (r. 22(1)(e))

5.2.7   Grandparents.
        (r. 22(1)(f))

5.2.8   Uncles or aunts of the whole blood or the issue of uncles or aunts of the whole blood who died before the deceased.
        (r. 22(1)(g))

5.2.9   Uncles or aunts of the half blood or the issue of uncles or aunts of the half blood who died before the deceased.
        (r. 22(1)(h))

5.2.10 If there is no-one in the above sections 5.2.1 to 5.2.9 who has an interest in the estate, the Treasury Solicitor is entitled to apply for a grant on behalf of the Crown.
        (r. 22(2))

5.2.11 In order for the Treasury Solicitor to be able to apply for a grant, he must claim "*bona vacantia*" (claim that the deceased died without kin entitled to the estate).

5.2.12 The term "the Crown" includes the Duchy of Lancaster and the Duke of Cornwall (r. 2(1)). See section 5.9 below for further details.

5.2.13 If there is no-one in sections 5.2.2 to 5.2.10 above willing to apply for a grant, a creditor or a person having no immediate beneficial interest in the estate but who would be entitled to a grant in the event of an accretion thereto (i.e. an increase in the value of the estate) may do so (r. 22(3)). See sections 5.3.8(a) and (b) and 5.10 below for further details.

5.2.14   The personal representative of any person in sections 5.2.2 to 5.2.9 above has the same right to a grant as the person for whom he is personal representative.
(r. 22(4))

5.2.15   5.2.14 above is subject to the limitation that any living person with an equal title with a person who is represented by a personal representative has prior title to the grant, unless the Registrar otherwise directs.
(r. 27(5))

5.3   Grant to surviving spouse

5.3.1   In order to be entitled to a grant, the survivor must have been the lawful spouse of the deceased (Administration of Estates Act 1925 (as amended s. 46).

5.3.2   The surviving spouse is not entitled to the whole of the estate unless:
(a) on dates of death on or after 1 June 1987, the net estate does not exceed £75,000.00 or
(b) on dates of death on or after 1 June 1987, the net estate exceeds £75,000.00 but does not exceed £125,000.00 and the deceased left no issue, or
(c) on dates of death on or after 1 June 1987, the net estate exceeds £125,000.00 and the deceased left no issue or parents or brothers or sisters of the whole blood or issue of predeceased brothers or sisters of the whole blood (Administration of Estates Act 1925 (as amended) s. 46).
For the amounts of the statutory legacy on dates of death prior to 1 June 1987, see paragraph 5.13 of the *Probate Manual*, 23rd edition.

5.3.3   Certain deductions are permitted in order to reduce the value of the net estate to ascertain whether a life interest arises (Administration of Estates Act 1925 (as amended) s. 46(1)(i)).

5.3.4   The deductions referred to in 5.3.3 above are:
(a) personal chattels
(b) Inheritance Tax
(c) costs incurred and to be incurred in the administration of the estate
(d) probate fees
(e) interest on the statutory legacy at the rate of 6% per annum (which rate applies on dates of death on or after 1 October 1983).

This is subject to the restriction that no sum is deductible if the actual interest on the whole estate exceeds the figure as described above (Administration of Estates Act 1925 (as amended) s. 46(4)) and Registrar's Direction 17 November 1960).

5.3.5   If the estate cannot be reduced to below the figures in section 5.3.2(b) above and the deceased left issue, then:
(a) the surviving spouse is entitled to the first £75,000.00 of the net estate, the personal goods and a life interest in one half of the remainder and the issue of the deceased are entitled to an equal share in the other half of the estate and to the surviving spouse's life interest on his or her death (Administration of Estates Act 1925 (as amended) s. 46(1)(i)(2))
(b) a life interest arises and two applicants are required unless the Registrar directs otherwise (Supreme Court Act 1981 s. 114(2))
(c) the applicants should be the surviving spouse and one of the children.

5.3.6   If the estate cannot be reduced to below the figures in section 5.3.2(c) above and the deceased left parents or brothers or sisters of the whole blood or the issue of predeceased brothers or sisters of the whole blood then:
(a) the surviving spouse is entitled to the first £125,000.00 of the net estate, the personal goods and chattels and one half of the remaining estate and the parents or the brothers or sisters of the whole blood or their issue (as the case may be) are entitled to share equally in the remaining half of the net estate;
(b) no life interest arises and only one applicant is required (Administration of Estates Act 1925 (as amended) s. 46(1)(i)(3)).

5.3.7   If the surviving spouse wishes to renounce in the event that a life interest arises and two applicants are required, two of the children of the deceased may take out the grant.

5.3.8   If all the children of the deceased are under 18 years of age, the surviving spouse may nominate someone to be the co-administrator. (r. 32(3))

5.3.9   In such cases, both a life and minority interest arises. For further details about minority interests, see Chapter 8.

5.3.10 (a) If the surviving spouse is entitled to the whole of the estate but wishes to renounce letters of administration, the issue of the deceased (or, if the deceased left no issue, the parents of the deceased, or if there are no parents, the brother or sister of the whole blood or the issue of predeceased brothers or sisters of the whole blood of the deceased) may take out the grant (r. 22(4)).

(b) The applicant's title to the grant is "a person who may have a beneficial interest in the estate in the event of an accretion thereto" (i.e. in the event that the value of the estate increases and exceeds the spouse's statutory legacy).

5.3.11 (a) If the surviving spouse is not entitled to the whole of the estate, upon his renunciation the other persons with a beneficial interest may take the grant.

(b) In the event that two applicants are required and there is only one willing and able to make the application (the other persons not being minors or mentally incapable), an application for a second administrator to be appointed should be made to the Registrar (r. 25(2)).

(c) A trust corporation may join in the application without such an order (r. 25(3)(b)).

(For further details on trust corporations, see Chapter 9.)

5.3.12 If the deceased's marriage was dissolved or annulled:

(a) the applicant for the grant should be the person with the highest priority next to the spouse under r. 22;

(b) the deceased is described as "a single woman" (or man, as the case may be);

(c) details of the decree should be recited in the oath, which should also include a statement that the deceased did not remarry.

5.3.13 On dates of death on or after 1 August 1970, a decree of judicial separation has the same effect upon the distribution of the estate and the entitlement to apply for a grant as a decree of divorce or annulment (Matrimonial Causes Act 1973, s. 18(2)).

5.3.14 In order to be effective, the decree of judicial separation must be subsisting at the date of death.

5.3.15 In certain circumstances, foreign decrees of divorce or separation are recognised in this country (Family Law Act 1986 Part II). For further details, see paragraphs 5.23ff of the *Probate Manual*, 23rd edition.

5.4 Grant to children

5.4.1 If the deceased left no surviving spouse, the grant may issue to the children of the deceased (r. 22(1)(b)).

5.4.2   The children may be lawful, legitimated, adopted or natural. All have equal title to the grant.

5.4.3   A grant may issue to the deceased's lawful children without supporting evidence as to their status.

5.4.4   A grant may issue to the natural child of a deceased mother without supporting evidence as to his relationship.

5.4.5   A grant may issue to the natural child of a deceased father if:
         (a) the date of death is on or after 1 January 1970 (Family Law Reform Act 1969 s. 14(1) on dates of death until 4 April 1988; Family Law Reform Act 1987 s. 18(1) on dates of death on or after 4 April 1988).
         (b) evidence can be produced to show that the deceased was the father of the child.

5.4.6   Section 5.4.5(b) above is no longer a requirement on dates of death on or after 4 April 1988.

5.4.7   Legitimated children have a right to a grant subject to such legitimation being established.

5.4.8   On dates of death on or after 4 April 1988 it is no longer necessary to establish legitimation (Family Law Reform Act 1987 s. 18).

5.4.9   Since 1 January 1976 legitimated children have overall the same rights as lawful children (Legitimacy Act 1976).

5.4.10   Since 1 January 1950, adopted children have an equal right to a grant in their adoptive parent's estate with other children as described in sections 5.4.3 to 5.4.8 above (dates of death prior to 1 January 1976 Adoption Act 1958 ss. 16 and 17; death on or after 1 January 1976, Children's Act 1975 Sch. 1, paragraph 3; and as from 1 January 1988 Adoption Act 1976 s. 39).

5.4.11   The adoption must have been in force at the date of death of the deceased.

5.4.12   Prior to 1 January 1950, succession rights were not affected by adoption.

5.4.13   Overseas adoptions can be recognised in certain circumstances. (For further details, see paragraph 5.36 of the *Probate Manual*, 23rd edition.)

5.4.14   Children of voidable marriages are treated as legitimate if born during the marriage (Matrimonial Causes Act 1973 s. 16).

5.4.15   On dates of death up until 4 April 1988 children of void marriages are treated as legitimate if:

    (a) either at the time of conception or, if later, the date of marriage of the parents, both or either of the parents reasonably believed the marriage to be valid, and

    (b) the child's father was domiciled in England and Wales at the date of the child's birth or, if the father died before the child's birth, at the date of the father's death (Legitimacy Act 1976 (as amended) s. 1).

5.4.16   In respect of dates of death on or after 4 April 1988, children of void marriages will be entitled to a grant of letters of administration in the estate of their parents if the provisions of s. 18 of the Family Law Reform Act 1987 apply.

5.4.17   In respect of dates of death on or after 4 April 1988, any child born as a result of artificial insemination is to be treated as a lawful child of the parties to the marriage regardless of whether the donor of the semen used in the insemination was the husband in the marriage if the husband consented to the insemination (Family Law Reform Act 1987 s. 27).

5.5   Grant to parents

5.5.1   If there is no surviving spouse or issue, the grant may issue to one or both of the parents of the deceased.

5.5.2   Adoptive parents have the same right to a grant as lawful parents if the deceased died after 1 January 1950 (dates of death up to 1 January 1976, Adoption Act 1958 s. 16(1); dates of death on or after 1 January 1976, Children Act 1975 Sch. 1, Part II; and as from 1 January 1988, Part IV of the Adoption Act 1976).

5.5.3   Natural parents of an illegitimate child have rights of succession to his estate.

5.5.4   The mother of a natural child has a right to a grant in his estate with no further evidence as to the facts being required (dates of death from 1 January 1927 but before 1 January 1970, Legitimacy Act 1926 s. 9(2); from 1 January 1970 but before 4 April 1988, Family Law Reform Act 1969 s. 14(2); and from 4 April 1988, Family Law Reform Act 1987 s. 18(1)).

5.5.5 (a) The father of a natural child has a right to a grant in its estate (dates of death from 1 January 1970 up to and including 3 April 1988, Family Law Reform Act 1969 s. 14(2); and on or after 4 April 1988, Family Law Reform Act 1987 s. 18(1)).

    (b) Evidence as to paternity of the child should be filed unless the date of death is on or since 4 April 1988, in which case no such evidence is normally required.

    (c) The evidence can take the form of a birth certificate which shows the father as the informant or if this cannot be produced, affidavit evidence supporting the applicant's claim to the satisfaction of the Registrar.

    (d) On dates of death prior to 1 January 1970, the natural father has no right to a grant or to a share in his child's estate.

5.6 Grant to brothers or sisters

5.6.1 If the deceased died without spouse, issue or parent, any brother or sister of the whole blood (i.e. with the same parents as the deceased) or the issue of any brother or sister of the whole blood who died before the deceased is entitled to the grant. (r. 22(1)(d))

5.6.2 (a) On dates of death up to and including 3 April 1988, the relationship to the deceased must be lawful to enable the application for the grant to be made (Administration of Estates Act 1925 (as amended) s. 46).

    (b) On dates of death on or after 4 April 1988, natural relationships are sufficient to pass title and such persons are equally entitled to a grant with persons lawfully related (Family Law Reform Act 1987 s. 18(1)).

    (c) There is no need to include either "lawful" or "natural" in the description of a relationship on dates of death on or after 4 April 1988, nor is there any need to lodge evidence as to paternity.

5.6.3 The issue of brothers or sisters of the whole blood who died before the deceased have equal title to a grant with brothers or sisters of the whole blood who survived the deceased (Administration of Estates Act 1925 (as amended) s. 47(3)).

5.6.4 The provisions of section 5.6.2 above apply to the issue of brothers or sisters of the whole blood who died before the deceased.

5.6.5 If the deceased died intestate without spouse, issue, parents or brothers or sisters of the whole blood (or the issue of any predeceased

brothers or sisters of the whole blood), any brother or sister of the half blood (i.e. having one parent in common with the deceased) or the issue of any brother or sister of the half blood who died before the deceased is entitled to a grant.
(r. 23(1)(e))

5.6.6 The provisions of sections 5.6.2 to 5.6.4 above apply equally to brothers and sisters of the half blood and the issue of predeceased brothers and sisters of the half blood.

5.7 Grant to grandparents

5.7.1 If the deceased died without spouse, issue, parent, brother or sister of the whole or half blood or the issue of any predeceased brothers or sisters of the whole or half blood, the grandparents of the deceased are entitled to a grant.
(r. 22(1)(f))

5.7.2 (a) On dates of death up to and including 3 April 1988, the grandparents must be lawfully related to the deceased (Administration of Estates Act 1925 (as amended) s. 46(1)(v)).
(b) On dates of death on or after 4 April 1988 natural grandparents and lawful grandparents have equal title to a grant (Family Law Reform Act 1987 s. 18(1)).

5.7.3 The provisions of section 5.6.2(c) above apply in respect of applications made by grandparents.

5.8 Grant to uncles or aunts

5.8.1 If the deceased died without spouse, issue, parent, brother or sister of the whole or half blood or the issue of any predeceased brother or sister of the whole or half blood, or grandparent, any uncle or aunt of the whole blood or the issue of any uncles or aunts of the whole blood who died before the deceased is entitled to a grant.
(r. 22(1)(g))

5.8.2 (a) On dates of death up to and including 3 April 1988 the uncle or aunt of the whole blood (or the issue of any predeceased uncles or aunts of the whole blood) must be lawfully related to the deceased (Administration of Estates Act 1925 (as amended) s. 46(1)(v)).

(b) On dates of death on or after 4 April 1988, natural uncles or aunts of the whole blood (or the issue of predeceased uncles or aunts of the whole blood) and lawful uncles or aunts of the whole blood or their issue have equal title to a grant (Family Law Reform Act 1987 s. 18(1)).

5.8.3 There is no need to include in the oath either "lawful" or "natural" in the description of the relationship in respect of uncles or aunts of the whole blood on dates of death on or after 4 April 1988 or any need to lodge evidence as to paternity.

5.8.4 Sections 5.6.3 and 5.8.3 above also apply to the issue of uncles or aunts of the whole blood.

5.8.5 If the deceased died without spouse, issue, parent, brother or sister of the whole or half blood or issue of any predeceased brothers or sisters of the whole or half blood, grandparent or uncle or aunt of the whole blood or the issue of any predeceased uncles or aunts of the whole blood, any uncle or aunt of the half blood or the issue of any uncles or aunts of the half blood who died before the deceased is entitled to a grant.
(r. 22(1)(h))

5.8.6 Sections 5.8.2 and 5.8.3 above apply to uncles and aunts of the half blood.

5.8.7 Section 5.8.4 above applies to the issue of uncles or aunts of the half blood who died in the lifetime of the deceased.

5.9 Grant to the Crown

5.9.1 If the deceased died without any person in sections 5.3 to 5.8 above surviving, the Crown is entitled to the grant.
(r. 22(2))

5.9.2 In order to apply for a grant, the Treasury Solicitor (who acts on behalf of the Crown) must claim "*bona vacantia*", i.e. that the deceased died without known kin.
(r. 22(2))

5.9.3 The Treasury Solicitor ("The Solicitor for the Affairs of Her Majesty's Treasury") includes for the purpose of the rules the solicitor for the affairs of the Duchy of Lancaster and the Solicitor of the Duchy of Cornwall.
(r. 2(1))

5.10 Grant to creditors

5.10.1   If all the persons entitled to a grant in sections 5.3 to 5.9 above have been cleared off, a creditor may take a grant, subject to section 5.10.2 below.
(r. 22(3))

5.10.2   (a) The persons referred to in Section 5.10.1 above may be cleared off by way of renunciation or citation.
(b) If no person in sections 5.3 to 5.8 above has survived the deceased, notice should be given to the Treasury Solicitor to ascertain whether he wishes to claim *bona vacantia* on behalf of the Crown (r. 38).
(c) If the Treasury Solicitor does not claim *bona vacantia* or renounces letters of administration, a grant may issue to a creditor.

5.10.3   If the creditor can swear only that the deceased died without *known* kin, then:
(a) a citation is usually issued citing any kin to accept or refuse a grant (see Chapter 16 for further details on citations).
(b) Notice should be given to the Treasury Solicitor (r. 38).

5.10.4   (a) If two applicants are required in the event that a life or minority interest arises, a further creditor or a trust corporation should join in the application (see r. 25(3)(b)).
(b) Application may be made to the Registrar to direct that the need for the second applicant be dispensed with (Supreme Court Act 1981 s. 114(2)).

5.10.5   (a) If a firm is a creditor, any of the partners (up to four in number) may make the application.
(b) In such cases, the oath should state that the remaining partners have consented to the application.

5.11   Grant to assignees

5.11.1   If all the persons entitled to share in the estate of the deceased assign their interest to another person or persons, the person to whom their interest is assigned takes their place in the order of priority under r. 22.
(r. 24(1))

5.11.2   Not all the assignees need join in the application but the consent of those not joining in is required in order to enable the grant to issue to the other or others.
(r. 24(2))

5.11.3   In the event that the estate exceeds the statutory legacy, the surviving spouse may apply for a grant as sole administrator if the other persons entitled to share in the estate of the deceased assign their interest to the spouse.

5.11.4   The deed of assignment should be lodged with the application for the grant together with a copy.
(r. 24(3))

5.12   Grant to personal representative

5.12.1   Subject to sections 5.12.2 and 5.12.3 below, the personal representative of any person in sections 5.3 to 5.8 and in section 5.10 above has the same right to a grant as the person whom he represents.
(r. 22(4))

5.12.2   The interest of a living person has priority over that of a personal representative of a deceased person who had equal title with the living person, unless the Registrar otherwise directs.
(r. 27(5))

5.12.3   The personal representative of a spouse who was not entitled to the whole estate of the deceased does *not* have a prior right to those persons who are entitled to share in the estate under sections 5.4 to 5.6 above.
(r. 22(4))

5.13   Special practice points to consider on the oath

5.13.1   Sections 3.2.5 to 3.2.8, 3.2.19 and 4.9.2 above all apply to the oath in respect of an application for letters of administration.

5.13.2   The clearing should set out all the classes in sections 5.3 to 5.8 above who have a prior right to the grant over the applicant, e.g. a lawful brother of the half blood applies on a date of death before 4 April 1988. The clearing is "a widow without issue or parent or brother or sister of the whole blood or their issue or any other person entitled in priority to share in her estate by virtue of any enactment".

5.13.3 (a) The applicant should include his relationship to the deceased in full, e.g. "lawful sister of the whole blood".

(b) On dates of death up to and including 3 April 1988 the word "lawful" must be included in respect of the applicant's relationship to the deceased save in applications where the relationship is of parent or child, in which case "natural" should be used if appropriate (Administration of Estates Act 1925 (as amended) s. 46).

(c) On dates of death on or after 4 April 1988 the word "lawful" need not be included in the applicant's title except in the case of the surviving spouse.

5.13.4 The words "or any other person entitled in priority to share in his/her estate by virtue of any enactment" should be added at the end of the clearing in respect of applications made in accordance with sections 5.5 to 5.10 (and 5.11 where appropriate) above (Family Law Reform Act 1969 s. 14). See section 5.13.2 above for an example. This wording is required in order to clear off any illegitimate children, adopted children, or children of a void marriage.

For further details in respect of the form of the oath, see the precedents following paragraph 5.49 in the *Probate Manual*, 23rd edition.

5.14   Miscellaneous points

5.14.1 If a life or minority interest arises (or may arise) in the deceased's estate, two applicants are required unless the Registrar otherwise directs or a trust corporation takes the grant (Supreme Court Act 1981 s. 114(2)).

5.14.2 (a) If, during the administration of an estate, a life or minority interest arises or continues and there is only one personal representative (such personal representative not being a trust corporation), application *may* be made to the Registrar to join an additional personal representative (Supreme Court Act 1981 s. 114(4)).

(b) The application is made to a Registrar and must be supported by an affidavit (r. 26(1)).

(c) The application may be made in respect of grants of probate and letters of administration (with will) as well as grants of letters of administration (Supreme Court Act 1981 s. 114(4) and (5)).

(d) The application can only be made in respect of estate *in which a grant has issued and is still subsisting* (Supreme Court Act 1981 s. 114(4)).

5.14.3   No grant of letters of administration may issue within 14 days of the date of death of the deceased unless a Registrar otherwise directs. (r. 6(2)).

5.14.4   A maximum number of four persons may obtain a grant of letters of administration (Supreme Court Act 1981, s. 114(1)).

5.14.5   (a) On dates of death up to and including 3 April 1988, an illegitimate child has only its parents as its next of kin and there is no other person entitled to a grant of letters of administration in respect of the estate (Family Law Reform Act 1969 s. 14).
         (b) On dates of death on or after 4 April 1988, any class of kin set out in sections 5.4 to 5.8 above is entitled to a grant of letters of administration of the estate of an illegitimate child in the order of priority in r. 22(1) (Family Law Reform Act 1987 s. 18(1)).

5.14.6   (a) Until 3 April 1988, the trustees or personal representatives could distribute the estate without ascertaining whether there were any persons entitled to share in the estate who could trace their relationship to the deceased by way of an illegitimate birth (Family Law Reform Act 1969 s. 17).
         (b) Since 4 April 1988, the protection in (a) above has been removed (Family Law Reform Act 1987 s. 20).

5.14.7   Unless the contrary can be shown, on dates of death on or after 4 April 1988, there is a presumption that the deceased has not been survived by:
         (a) any person whose parents were not married to each other at the time of his birth, nor
         (b) anyone who is related to him by way of (a) above (Family Law Reform Act 1982 s. 21).

5.14.8   (a) On dates of death from 1 January 1970 up to and including 3 April 1988, an illegitimate child is presumed not to have been survived by his father unless the contrary can be shown (Family Law Reform Act 1969 s. 14(4)).
         (b) On dates of death on or after 4 April 1988, (a) above still applies with the addition that the presumption of non-survival is extended to cover any person related to the deceased solely through his father (Family Law Reform Act 1987 s. 18(2)).

6. Inland Revenue Accounts and Inheritance Tax

Contents

6.1 Introduction

6.1.1   There is a general requirement that a certificate in the form of an Inland Revenue account is required to be lodged when an application for a grant is made. The account should state either that inheritance tax payable on the delivery of the account has been paid or that there is no inheritance tax payable. This must be done before the grant can issue (Supreme Court Act 1981 s. 109(1)).

6.1.2   There is one exception to 6.1.1 above and this is described in section 6.3 below.

6.2 Delivery of the Inland Revenue account

6.2.1   (a) If inheritance tax is payable, the personal representatives may give notice to the Inland Revenue that they wish to defer payment on certain types of property (Inheritance Tax Act 1984 ss. 227–9).

(b) The inheritance tax payable on instalment option property should be paid before the issue of the grant (Inheritance Tax Act 1984 s. 228).

(For details as to what is counted as instalment and non-instalment option property, see Chapter 6, paragraphs 6.53–4 of the *Probate Manual*, 23rd edition).

PPN– D

6.2.2   Unless the estate is an "excepted estate" and falls within the ambit of the Capital Transfer Tax (Delivery of Account) Regulations 1981, as amended, an Inland Revenue account is required.

6.3   Excepted estates

6.3.1   On dates of death since 1 April 1981 it is not necessary on certain small estates for an Inland Revenue account to be filed (Capital Transfer Tax (Delivery of Account) Regulations 1981, as amended).

6.3.2   An Inland Revenue account is not required to be delivered on estates when the deceased died on or after 1 April 1981 if:
   (a) the deceased's property consists entirely of assets which pass under the grant or by way of nomination or by survivorship to another joint owner,
   (b) the total gross value of the property in (a) above does not exceed £25,000 (but see 6.3.3 and 6.3.5–7 below),
   (c) not more than 10% of the total gross value or £1,000 (whichever is the higher) consists of property situated out of the United Kingdom,
   (d) the deceased died domiciled in the United Kingdom and did not make any chargeable transfers during his lifetime (Regulation 3, Capital Transfer Tax (Delivery of Account Regulations) 1981).

6.3.3   On 1 September 1983, the Capital Transfer Tax (Delivery of Account) (no. 3) Regulations 1983 made the following amendments to section 6.3.2 above:
   (a) the figure in (b) was amended to £40,000
   (b) the figure in (c) was amended to £2,000.

6.3.4   The figures in 6.3.3 above apply to dates of death on or since 1 April 1983.

6.3.5   On 1 August 1987, the Inheritance Tax (Delivery of Account) Regulations 1987 further amended the regulations in section 6.3.2 above.

6.3.6   The regulations in section 6.3.5 above made the following amendments:
   (a) the figure in (b) of 6.3.2 above (as amended) was further amended to £70,000;
   (b) the limitation in (c) of 6.3.2 above (as amended) (in respect of both the figure and the percentage) was replaced by the figure of £10,000.

6.3.7   The amendments in 6.3.6 above apply to dates of death on or since 1 April 1987.

6.3.8   If sections 6.3.2, 6.3.3 and 6.3.6 above apply, the case is known as an "excepted estate" and no Inland Revenue account need be filed.

6.3.9   The gross figure in the oath should be in accordance with the appropriate regulations (bearing in mind the date of death) and it should be stated that the estate "does not exceed" the appropriate figure.

6.3.10   The question as to whether the estate is an excepted estate is governed by the regulations in force at the date of death and *not* by those in force at the date of the application for the grant.

6.3.11   The net estate should be shown on the oath as "does not exceed £10,000" (£25,000, £40,000 or £70,000 as appropriate and in accordance with the regulations in force at the date of death).

6.3.12   In an excepted estate, the figures shown for the net estate govern the fee payable under the fees order in force at the date of the application (at present the Non-Contentious Probate Fees Order 1981 as amended) and are used solely for the purpose of calculating the fee.

6.3.13   The statement that the estate is not one in which an Inland Revenue account is required to be delivered must be included in the oath.

6.3.14   It should be noted that for the purpose of ascertaining whether the estate is an excepted estate, only the deceased's share in any joint property need be included in the calculation.

6.3.15   Where a second grant issues in an estate in which a full grant has already issued (and that estate was an "excepted estate") it may remain an "excepted estate" and the appropriate "band" figures should then be included in the oath.

6.3.16   A limited grant (such as an *ad colligenda bona* grant) may be treated as an "excepted estate" and, if appropriate, may continue to be dealt with as an "excepted estate" when the application for the full grant is made.

EXCEPTED ESTATES
on which an Inland Revenue account does not need to be filed

Date of death	Total gross value of estate does not exceed	Limit on property situated outside the UK
1.4.81–31.3.83	£25,000	Not more than higher of 10% or £1,000
1.4.83–31.3.87	£40,000	Not more than higher of 10% or £2,000
1.4.87–	£70,000	Not more than £10,000

The conditions in section 6.3.2 (a) and (d) must also be satisfied.

6.4   Correct form of Inland Revenue account

6.4.1   In every case in which sections 6.3.2, 6.3.3 and 6.3.6 do not apply, an Inland Revenue account (or affidavit) is required (Supreme Court Act 1981 s. 109(1)).

6.4.2   The one exception to section 6.4.1 above is dealt with in sections 13.8.1–13.8.3 below.

6.4.3   There are various forms of account which are appropriate to different types of application.

6.4.4   Cap form 200 should be used if:
(a) the deceased died on or after 27 March 1981 domiciled in the United Kingdom;
(b) inheritance tax is payable;
(c) Cap form 202 (see section 6.4.6 below) is not suitable for some other reason.

6.4.5   Cap form 201 should be used if the deceased died domiciled out of the United Kingdom.

6.4.6   Cap form 202 should be used if:
(a) the deceased died on or after 27 March 1981 domiciled in the United Kingdom;
(b) all the deceased's property was situated in the United Kingdom

and consisted entirely of property passing under the grant, by way of nomination or of joint property passing by survivorship;

(c) no inheritance tax is payable;

(d) within 10 years of his death, and after 26 March 1974, the deceased made no chargeable transfers (i.e. chargeable to capital transfer tax).

6.4.7 Cap form A-5C should be used if the application is a second or subsequent grant in respect of the property covered by the first grant. Such cases are:

(a) double probate (see section 3.3 above)

(b) *de bonis non* (see section 10.1 below)

(c) cessate grants (see section 10.7 below).

6.4.8 In all cases other than those in section 6.4.7 above, the form in sections 6.4.2 to 6.4.6 above should be used. Earlier prints of the forms are available to cover dates of death before 27 March 1981.

6.4.9 Supplies of all the forms in sections 6.4.4 to 6.4.7 above can be obtained from the Capital Taxes Office, Minford House, Rockley Road, London W14 0DF.

6.5 Miscellaneous points

6.5.1 Since 13 March 1975 no inheritance tax has been payable on transfers between a deceased and the surviving spouse (Inheritance Tax Act 1984 s. 18).

6.5.2 The current figure above which inheritance tax is payable is £110,000 on dates of death on or since 15 March 1988 (Finance Act 1988).

6.5.3 On dates of death before 13 March 1975 an Inland Revenue affidavit sworn by the applicants for the grant is required to be lodged.

6.5.4 On dates of death on or since 13 March 1975 an Inland Revenue account signed by the applicants for the grant is required to be lodged (unless the estate is an "excepted estate").

6.5.5 Cap forms 201 and A-5C must be sent to the Capital Taxes Office to be controlled before the papers to lead to the grant are lodged.
(For an outline of inheritance tax, examples of accounts and the rates of inheritance tax, see Chapter 6 of the *Probate Manual*, 23rd edition.)

7. Foreign Domicile

Contents

7.1 Foreign domicile – introduction

7.1.1 The domicile of the deceased governs the form in which the application is made for the grant. Applications in respect of persons who died domiciled out of England and Wales are made under r. 30.

7.1.2 For the purposes of domicile out of England and Wales, rr. 20, 22, 25 and 27 do not apply, save in relation to r. 30(3) (r. 28(2)). See sections 7.5.4 to 7.5.6 below for further details in respect of r. 30(3).

7.1.3 Evidence as to the law of any country outside England and Wales may be given by way of an affidavit sworn by a person qualified in that law or someone whose knowledge and experience may enable the Registrar to accept his evidence.
(r. 19(a))

7.1.4 Evidence as set out in section 7.1.3 above may also be given by way of a certificate by or act made before a notary practising in the country of domicile.
(r. 19(b))

7.2 Validity of the will – date of death before 1 January 1964

7.2.1 In respect of dates of death before 1 January 1964, the rule is that usually a will is capable of proof in England and Wales if it has been accepted as valid by the court having jurisdiction at the place where the deceased died domiciled (*re Yahuda* [1956] P 388).

.2.2   The will of a British subject made before 1 January 1964 may be regarded as valid in respect of personal estate and admissible to proof in England and Wales if:

(a) it is executed out of the United Kingdom and has been made in accordance with and is formally valid by the law of the place where it was made, or by the law of the place of domicile of the deceased at its execution, or by the law of the deceased's domicile of origin, or

(b) it is executed in the United Kingdom and is formally valid by the law then in force in the part of the United Kingdom where it was executed (Wills Act 1861 ss. 1 & 2).

.2.3   Grants made in respect of section 7.2.2 above are limited to personalty.

.2.4   That part of a will executed before 1 January 1964 which exercises a power of appointment is capable of proof if the will was executed in accordance with the Wills Act 1837 (Wills Act 1837 s. 10).

.2.5   If a will is to be proved in accordance with section 7.2.1 above, an office or similar copy issued by the Court in which it has been proved should be lodged and marked in accordance with section 3.2.3 above.

.2.6   If a will is in English form and the deceased died domiciled in Northern Ireland, the Republic of Ireland, Australia, New Zealand or Canada, it can be accepted for proof without evidence as to its validity (Registrar's Direction 20 November 1972).

.2.7   A will is capable of proof in England and Wales if it was made in accordance with the law of the place where the deceased was domiciled either at the date of its execution, or the date of his death.

.3   Validity of the will – date of death on or after 1 January 1964

.3.1   The validity of the will of a person who died on or after 1 January 1964 (whether or not it was made before or after that date) is governed by the Wills Act 1963 (see section 2.9 above).

.3.2   Basically, the provisions in sections 7.2.1, 7.2.5, 7.2.6 and 7.2.7 above also apply to dates of death on or after 1 January 1964 but have been extended by the Wills Act 1963.

7.3.3   If it is desired to establish the will's validity by way of the deceased's nationality, and more than one system of internal law may apply care must be taken to set out the basis upon which the claim in respect of the deceased's closest connection with the internal law of the country of which he is a national is founded as fully as possible.

7.3.4   It should be noted that the Wills Act 1861 was repealed in its entirety by the Wills Act 1963 when the latter came into force but is still effective in respect of dates of death before 1 January 1964.

7.4   Practice points regarding the proof of wills

7.4.1   The original will should be lodged and marked in accordance with r. 10 if it is available.

7.4.2   If the original will is not available and is held by a foreign court (whether or not it has been proved by that court) or official, a certified copy issued by the court or official will be admitted to proof by the court in England and Wales without an order.
(r. 54(2))

7.4.3   If the will is not held as set out in section 7.4.2 above, an order by the Registrar to admit a copy will to proof is required.
(r. 54(1))

7.4.4   If the will is in a language other than English, a translation should be lodged with the original when the application is made for the grant or on any earlier reference to the court.

7.4.5   The translation should be certified as accurate by an English notary or a British consular official of the country involved.

7.4.6   If a certified translation as set out in 7.4.5 above is not available, a translator qualified in and conversant with the language of the will may make the translation, but the acceptability of this is at the discretion of the Registrar and an affidavit by the translator setting out his qualifications and experience in translating legal documents may be required.

7.4.7   If the will is made in two languages (e.g. English and Spanish), translation in accordance with sections 7.4.5 or 7.4.6 above should be prepared in respect of the foreign language part of the will.

7.4.8   (a) The validity of the will in accordance with sections 7.2 and 7. above should be established by way of evidence relevant to the case, bearing in mind the provisions of r. 19.

(b) However, evidence as required in (a) above will not be necessary if the will was made before a notary in the country of domicile, retained by him (or his successor) in his records and the copy supplied for proof was issued by him (Practice Direction [1972] 3 All ER 1019).

7.4.9 It should be noted that the original will (or the certified copy thereof) and not the translation should be marked in accordance with r. 10.

7.5 Application for a grant

7.5.1 The entitlement to a grant in respect of the estate of a person who died domiciled abroad is governed by r. 30.

7.5.2 The persons entitled to apply for a grant under r. 30 are as follows:
(a) the person entrusted with the administration of the estate by the law of the deceased's domicile (r. 30(1)(a))
(b) when there is no person in (a) above, the person beneficially entitled to the estate of the deceased by the law of his domicile (r. 30(1)(b))
(c) such person as the Registrar thinks fit in all the surrounding circumstances (r. 30 (1)(c))
(d) if the will is in English or Welsh and is admissible to proof in England and Wales, the executor named therein (r. 30(3)(a)(i)), or if the duties are sufficiently described in the will, the executor according to the tenor (i.e. terms) of the will (r. 30(3)(a)(ii))
(e) if the whole or substantially the whole of the estate in England and Wales consists of immovable estate, to the person entitled to a grant in accordance with the law of England and Wales (r. 30(3)(b)).

7.5.3 Section 7.5.2(a)–(c) above requires an order of the Registrar made under the relevant part of the Rule before the grant can issue.

7.5.4 If an application is contemplated under section 7.5.2(d) above, it should be noted that it is not possible to accept an appointment of an executor in a language other than English or Welsh unless the duties are sufficiently clearly defined within the terms of the will to enable the person so appointed to be identified as an executor in accordance with the terms thereof ("executor according to the tenor of the will").

7.5.5 The Rule in section 7.5.2(d) above is interpreted by the court as including an application for the grant by the attorney of the executor.

7.5.6   The right to a grant as executor applies even if the executor appointed by the will would not be entitled to a grant of probate in England and Wales (e.g. a non-trust corporation), although such an application can only be made by way of an attorney or nominee.

7.5.7   An application in accordance with section 7.5.2(a) above is made when a court in the country of the deceased's domicile has issued a document entrusting the administration of the estate to a named person or organisation.

7.5.8   Generally speaking, documents taking the form of grants of representation are entrusting documents but any document issued by the court of domicile which entrusts the administration of the estate may be sufficient to enable the Registrar to make the order.

7.5.9   The entrusting document should be lodged with the application for the grant together with a translation if the document is in a foreign language.

7.5.10 In such applications, no affidavit of law is required either in respect of the applicant's title to the grant or to establish the validity of the will if it has been proved in the country of domicile.

7.5.11 The grant is always one of letters of administration or letters of administration (with will).

7.5.12 If a life or minority interest arises in the estate and there is only one person entrusted with the administration, the Registrar may, by order, join another administrator with the person so entrusted. (r. 30(2))

7.5.13 If there is no person entrusted with the administration of the estate, the grant may issue in accordance with section 7.5.2(b) above.

7.5.14 In order to identify the person entitled to a beneficial interest in the estate, evidence of the law of the country of the deceased's domicile should be lodged.

7.5.15 If there has been no order or decision of the court of domicile as to the beneficial interest in the estate, the evidence required by section 7.5.14 above may either take the form of an affidavit sworn by an expert in that law or a certificate by or act made before a notary practising in the country of domicile. (r. 19)

7.5.16 If there are facts upon which the foreign law expert has relied when making his affidavit, the truth of such facts must be verified by way of inclusion in the oath to lead to the grant or by way of separate affidavit.

7.5.17 In the event that the applicant is not the only person entitled to a beneficial interest in the estate, the Registrar may direct to whom, amongst those persons, the grant may issue.
(r. 30(1)(b))

7.5.18 It should be noted that a grant may issue in accordance with section 7.5.2(b) above notwithstanding that the country of domicile is one which usually issues grants of representation, provided that no such grant has issued.

7.5.19 It is open to the Registrar to make an order under section 7.5.2(c) above at his discretion.

7.5.20 An application for an order as in section 7.5.19 above requires an affidavit of facts and evidence of the law of domicile to be lodged to enable the Registrar to make the order before the application for the grant is made.

7.5.21 The affidavit of facts referred to in section 7.5.20 above should contain all the relevant details of the application, the reason it is desired that the Registrar should exercise his discretion, the gross and net values of the estate in England and Wales and a request for the order.

7.5.22 Once the order has been made, the application for the grant may be lodged. The oath should recite details of the date and place of the order and by whom it was made.

7.5.23 In the case of an application under section 7.5.2(e) above, no evidence of foreign law is required and the oath should contain the clearing and title as for a similar case in which the deceased died domiciled in England and Wales.

7.5.24 It should be noted that r. 30(3)(b) applies English law to all aspects of the application, including the question of whether a life or minority interest arises.

7.5.25 If the estate in England and Wales does not consist wholly of immovable property, reference should be made to the Registrar to confirm that he is prepared to allow the application on the basis that the estate in England and Wales consists substantially of immovable estate.

7.5.26   It is of assistance in applications under section 7.5.25 above if a breakdown of the estate can be supplied.

7.6   Special practice points to consider on the oath

7.6.1   Details of the applicant and the deceased should be recited in the oath as set out in Chapters 3, 4 and 5 as appropriate.

7.6.2   The existence of a life and minority interest and whether settled land is involved should be included in the oath in the same manner as in other applications.

7.6.3   The deceased's domicile should be stated as either the country in which he was domiciled or, in cases in which the country has states which have different systems of law (e.g. Australia, United States of America), the state in which he was domiciled.

7.6.4   The title of the applicant under r. 30(1) should be included in the oath (e.g. "the person entrusted with the administration of the estate of the deceased by the court having jurisdiction at the place where the deceased died domiciled" (r. 30(1)(a); "the person beneficially entitled to the estate of the deceased by the law of the place where the deceased died domiciled" (r. 30(1)(b)) and details of any order obtained recited.

7.6.5   If the application is made by the attorney of the person entitled to apply, care must be taken to include the limitation "until further representation be granted" after the promise to administer in the oath. If any additional form of limitation is used, this should be similarly included.

7.6.6   The gross and net values of the estate shown on the oath should be those appertaining to the estate in England and Wales and should be described as such.
        For further details in respect of the form of the oath, see the precedents following paragraph 7.29 of the *Probate Manual*, 23rd edition.

7.7   Miscellaneous points

7.7.1   If the deceased died domiciled in Scotland or Northern Ireland and a grant has been obtained in that country showing the domicile, the document obtained is sufficient to enable the English assets to be administered without a further grant being required (Administration of Estates Act 1971 s. 1).

7.7.2   Reciprocal provisions apply in respect of English grants in Scotland and Northern Ireland (Administration of Estates Act 1971 ss. 2 and 3).

7.7.3   If the deceased died domiciled in Scotland or Northern Ireland and no grant has issued in that country, it is possible to obtain a grant in England and Wales, but the grant will be limited to estate in England and Wales and until representation be granted in the country of domicile.

7.7.4   In the case of an application under section 7.7.3 above, the validity of any will has to be established in the manner set out in section 7.2 or 7.3 above.

7.7.5   It is possible for a will which could not be proved in the country of the deceased's domicile to be admissible to proof in England and Wales if its validity can be established by way of the Wills Act 1963.

7.7.6   Translations of wills in the Welsh language may be obtained from the Probate Registry of Wales (see section 1.4.3 above for the address) upon payment of the appropriate fee.

7.7.7   The deceased's domicile does not normally have to be substantiated to the satisfaction of the Probate Registries beyond the sworn statement in the affidavit/oath, but a statement of domicile must be included in the Inland Revenue account.

7.7.8   An Inland Revenue account is always necessary in cases in which the deceased has died domiciled out of the United Kingdom and should be controlled by the Capital Taxes Office before application is made for the grant.

7.7.9   A renunciation executed in respect of an application made in a foreign court is not acceptable in proceedings in England and Wales. If it is desired to renounce effectively in an application made in England and Wales, a further renunciation should be executed.

7.7.10   It is not possible to obtain a grant in England and Wales if the deceased did not leave any estate in this country unless it is to deal with trust property (*Aldrich v Attorney-General* [1968] P 281).

7.7.11   Resealing a foreign grant is an alternative to an application under r. 30.
          See Chapter 12 for further details.

8. Grants for the use of Minors, for Persons under a Mental Disability and to Attorneys

GRANTS FOR THE USE OF MINORS

8.1 Introduction

8.1.1 If the person entitled to administer the estate of the deceased is under the age of 18 years, a grant for his use and benefit until he attains that age may issue in accordance with r. 32.

8.1.2 If there is more than one minor involved, the grant is limited until one of them attains the age of 18 years.
(r. 32(1))

8.1.3   The following persons may apply for a grant under r. 32(1):
      (a) the parents of a minor *jointly*
      (b) the statutory guardian
      (c) the testamentary guardian
      (d) a guardian appointed by a court of competent jurisdiction.

8.1.4   Grants for the use and benefit of a sole minor executor having no interest in the residuary estate are made to a residuary legatee or devisee and limited in accordance with sections 8.1.1 and 8.1.2 above. (r. 32(1))

8.1.5   If a minor is only one of the executors, probate may be granted to the other executors able to apply with power reserved to the minor executor. (r. 33(1))

8.1.6   In the circumstances of section 8.1.5 above, application to the Registrar should be made to dispense with service of notice of the application upon the minor executor. (r. 27(3))

8.1.7   If all other executors who are not minors have renounced probate or have been cited to take a grant but have not done so, letters of administration (with will) may issue for the use and benefit of the minor executor in accordance with r. 32. (r. 33(2))

8.2   Persons entitled to apply for a grant

8.2.1   If a minority interest arises, two applicants are required unless a trust corporation applies or a Registrar otherwise directs (Supreme Court Act 1981 s. 114(2)).

8.2.2   If there is more than one branch of a family entitled to apply for a grant, it is not essential to have a representative from each branch, although such a course of action is desirable.

8.2.3   If there is only one person entitled to a grant for the use of the minor, he or she may nominate a co-administrator to join in the application. (r. 32(3))

8.2.4   It should be noted that a person of full age will be preferred to the representatives of a minor who has equal title unless the Registrar otherwise directs. (r. 27(5))

8.2.5   Application in respect of section 8.1.3(a) above must be made by both parents jointly.

8.2.6   If the minor entitled to the grant has only one lawful parent surviving, that parent is the minor's statutory guardian (Guardianship of Minors Act 1971 s. 3(1) and (2)).

8.2.7   If the minor is illegitimate, the surviving parent is not the statutory guardian unless an order has been made under s. 9(1) of the Guardianship of Minors Act 1971. In such cases, upon the death of the mother, the father becomes the statutory guardian (Guardianship of Minors Act 1971 s. 3).

8.2.8   If the minor is an adopted child, the adoptive parents are entitled to apply jointly for a grant in the same manner as set out in section 8.1.3 above (Adoption Act 1976, Part IV).

8.2.9   (a) The surviving parent of the joint adoptive parents is the minor's statutory guardian (Adoption Act 1976, Part IV).
          (b) This does not apply if the minor was adopted by one parent only (see Guardianship of Minors Act 1971 s. 3).

8.2.10   A testamentary guardian is appointed either by the mother or father of the child and the appointment takes effect at the death of the person appointing.

8.2.11   The mother of an illegitimate child may appoint a testamentary guardian in respect of her child. The father may do so if he was entitled to a custody order under s. 9 of the Guardianship of Minors Act 1971.

8.2.12   The court may appoint a person guardian of a minor under certain circumstances (Guardianship of Minors Act 1971 s. 5(1)).

8.2.13   If there is no person willing and able to take a grant as set out in section 8.1.3 above, the Registrar may assign guardians to a minor for the purpose of extracting a grant.
          (r. 32(2))

8.2.14   The Registrar may assign a guardian to act jointly with or to the exclusion of anyone in section 8.1.3 above.
          (r. 32(3))

8.2.15   If a minor is in the care of a local authority under s. 3 of the Child Care Act 1980, that authority may take out a grant on behalf of the minor as its guardian.

8.2.16   In certain circumstances, the local authority may act as a trust corporation and take out the grant in its own right (Public Trustee Rules 1912; Public Trustee (Custodian Trustee) Rules 1971 (as amended)).

8.2.17   Generally speaking, the local authority can only act as a trust corporation if the property in the deceased's estate devolves solely upon the child in care. (See Chapter 9 for further details on trust corporations.)

8.2.18   If the local authority cannot act as a trust corporation, its nominees may take out the grant. (See Chapter 9 for further details on non-trust corporations.)

8.2.19   In cases under sections 8.2.16 and 8.2.18 above, an order of the Registrar under r. 32(2) is required (Registrar's Direction 30 June 1976).

8.2.20   Similar considerations to sections 8.2.15 to 8.2.19 apply in respect of children who are subject to a care order under the Children and Young Persons Act 1969.

8.3   Procedure in applications in respect of minors

8.3.1   If an order of the Registrar is required to assign a guardian or guardians, an ex-parte application supported by an affidavit of facts should be lodged for consideration.

8.3.2   The affidavit should contain all the facts regarding the deceased and the applicant, the reason for requiring the order and should make application for the order in terms. Any relevant supporting documents should be exhibited.

8.3.3   If the minor's title depends upon the fact that the deceased was divorced, it is no longer necessary to file an office copy of the decree absolute with the application for the grant unless the divorce was granted out of England and Wales.

8.3.4   Any court orders or resolutions upon which the applicant relies should be lodged with the application under r. 32 or, if no order is required, with the application for the grant.

8.3.5   The order assigning guardians referred to in section 8.3.1 above is usually obtained before the oath to lead to the grant is sworn.

8.3.6   An oath (and, depending upon the estate, an Inland Revenue account) is required to obtain the grant.

8.4   Special practice points to consider on the oath

8.4.1   The oath in support of the application for the grant takes the general form of those in sections 4.5 and 9.13 above.

8.4.2   If the deceased was divorced, details of the divorce decree, including the date of the decree absolute and the court where it was made and the fact that he or she did not remarry, should be included in the oath.

8.4.3   Details of any order obtained (usually orders of the Registrar assigning a guardian or guardians) should be included in the oath.

8.4.4   Save in the case of a minor executor having no interest in the estate, a minority interest always arises in these applications and the oath should be completed accordingly.

8.4.5   The appropriate limitation (see section 8.1.2 above) should be included after the promise to administer.
          For further details and examples of oaths, see the precedents after paragraph 8.24 of the *Probate Manual*, 23rd edition.

8.5   Miscellaneous points

8.5.1   In the case of a deceased who died domiciled out of England and Wales where the minors entitled to the grant are domiciled in England and Wales, English law determines who the representatives of the minor shall be, but the law of the domicile governs the identity of the person entitled to the grant.

8.5.2   In the case of a deceased who died domiciled in England and Wales where the minors entitled to the grant are domiciled out of England and Wales, the law of the domicile of the minors determines who shall act on their behalf and the law of England and Wales governs whether these persons shall be entitled to take out the grant.

8.5.3   The right of a minor executor to a grant of probate cannot be renounced by someone acting on his behalf in any capacity.
          (r. 34(1))

8.5.4   A Registrar may assign a guardian specifically for the purpose of renouncing a minor's right to a grant of administration. (r. 34(2))

8.5.5   If the minor is a ward of court, the Registrar to whom the case is assigned or the judge who is dealing with the matter should be requested to give directions in respect of the application.

GRANTS FOR THE USE OF PERSONS UNDER A MENTAL DISABILITY

8.6   Introduction

8.6.1   Grants on behalf of persons suffering from mental incapacity are issued pursuant to r. 35.

8.6.2   Before such an application can be made, persons who have equal title to the grant with the incapable person must be cleared off, unless the Registrar directs otherwise. (r. 35(1))

8.6.3   The order of priority for a grant of administration for the use and benefit of the mentally incapable person is as follows:
   (a) the person authorised to apply for a grant by the Court of Protection (r. 35(2)(a))
   (b) if there is no-one authorised in (a) above, the lawful attorney appointed by the incapable person under a registered enduring power of attorney (r. 35(2)(b))
   (c) in the absence of any person entitled in (a) and (b) above, the person entitled to the residuary estate of the deceased may apply for a grant (r. 35(2)(c)).

8.6.4   The Registrar has discretion to issue a grant to two or more persons (up to a maximum of four), whether or not there is anyone qualified in section 8.6.3 above. (r. 35(4))

8.6.5   In all applications under sections 8.6.3(b) and (c) and 8.6.4 above, notice of the application must be given to the Court of Protection (r. 35(5)). See section 1.5.7 for the address to which the notice should be sent.

8.6.6   If the application is made under section 8.6.3(c) or 8.6.4 above, medical evidence confirming the incapable person's mental incapacity should be lodged with the papers to lead to the Registrar's order or, if no order is required, with the papers to lead to the grant.

8.7   Persons entitled to apply for a grant

8.7.1   To be entitled to a grant under section 8.6.3(a) above, the applicant must have obtained an order authorising him to apply for a grant on behalf of the incapable person from the Court of Protection under the Mental Health Act 1983.

8.7.2   If two applicants are required and only one person has been authorised in the order from the Court of Protection, the person so named may nominate a co-administrator to act jointly with him. (r. 35(3))

8.7.3   To be able to apply under section 8.6.3(b) above, the power of attorney must have been registered in the Court of Protection.

8.7.4   If there is only one attorney willing and able to apply for a grant, the person so appointed may nominate a co-administrator to join in the application. (r. 35(4))

8.7.5   Applications under section 8.6.3(c) above can be made by any residuary beneficiary on behalf of the incapable person.

8.7.6   If there is only one residuary beneficiary willing and able to take a grant, he may nominate a co-administrator to join in the application. (r. 35(4))

8.7.7   It should be noted that an application under section 8.6.4 above may not be made by an individual. The Registrar only has discretion to appoint two or more (up to a maximum of four) persons as administrators.

8.7.8   Application for an order under section 8.6.4 above is made ex-parte to the Registrar, supported by an affidavit of facts which should include all the details of the deceased, the incapable person and the applicants and should include the reasons for requiring the order. Any documents in support of the application should be exhibited.

8.7.9   The order is usually obtained before the oath to lead to the grant is sworn.

8.8   Special practice points to consider on the oath

8.8.1   The oath should be in the appropriate form as set out in sections 4.5 and 9.13 above.

8.8.2 The existence of an order of priority in r. 35 necessitates that those persons with a prior right to the grant to that of the applicant be cleared off on the oath (e.g. on an application under section 8.6.3(c) above, the oath should state that there is no person authorised by the Court of Protection to take a grant and that there is no lawful attorney of the incapable person acting under a registered enduring power of attorney).

8.8.3 It is not necessary to clear persons with a prior right to the applicant if the Registrar has made an order under r. 35(4).

8.8.4 If a nomination has been made in accordance with r. 35(3), details of this should be recited in the oath and the nomination lodged.

8.8.5 Details of any order of the Registrar should be recited in the oath.

8.8.6 The limitation "for the use and benefit of (the incapable person) and until further representation be granted", together with any additional words of limitation directed by the Registrar, should be included after the promise to administer on the oath.

For examples of the forms of oath, see the precedents following paragraph 8.39 of the *Probate Manual*, 23rd edition.

8.9 Miscellaneous points

8.9.1 If there is someone not under a disability who has an equal title to the grant with the mentally incapable person, the former shall be preferred as an applicant to the representative of the latter, unless the Registrar otherwise directs.
(r. 35(1))

8.9.2 If one executor out of two or more is mentally incapable, the grant of probate may issue to the other executors with power reserved to the incapable executor.

8.9.3 In the case of section 8.9.2 above, before the papers to lead to the grant are sworn, application should be made to the Registrar to dispense with the service of notice of the application for probate upon the incapable executor.
(r. 27(3))

8.9.4 It should be noted that there is no specific authority to issue grants in respect of persons suffering from a physical incapacity. Such applications can be made under section 8.10 below.

8.9.5   The evidence in respect of the incapacity of the incapable person
          should take the form of a letter from the responsible medical officer
          if the incapable person is resident in hospital or nursing home, or
          from the incapable person's G.P. if he or she is not so resident. It
          should set out the patient's name, state that he or she is resident in
          an institution (if it be the case) and, in the opinion of the person so
          certifying, is incapable of managing his or her affairs by reason of
          mental incapacity and is likely to remain so for a period of at least
          three months.

8.9.6   The acknowledgement of the notice served upon the Court of
          Protection in accordance with section 8.6.5 above should be lodged
          with the application for the grant.

GRANTS TO ATTORNEYS

8.10   Introduction

8.10.1   A person entitled to a grant of representation and who is not under a
          disability may appoint an attorney to take out the grant for his use
          and benefit until further representation be granted.
          (r. 31)

8.10.2   The attorney may be a named individual or individuals or a trust
          corporation.

8.10.3   The attorney appointed acts on behalf of the donor of the attorney
          and administers the estate until either his death, the death of the
          donor, or until a further grant issues.
          (r. 31(1))

8.11   Practice on applications for attorney grants

8.11.1   It is not necessary for a person to reside out of England and Wales
          before he can appoint an attorney. There is no restriction to prevent
          anyone with a title to a grant who resides in England and Wales from
          appointing an attorney.
          (r. 31(1))

8.11.2   Anyone with a title to a grant may appoint an attorney to take out the
          grant on his behalf, but if an executor appoints an attorney, notice of
          the application for the grant should be given to the other executors,
          unless the Registrar otherwise directs.
          (r. 31(2))

8.11.3   The power of attorney may be executed out of England and Wales, but if the place of execution is a non English-speaking country and the power of attorney is in English, evidence that the donor understands the English language is required.

8.11.4   If the power of attorney is in a foreign language, an acceptable translation should be lodged.

8.11.5   If a life or minority interest arises, the donor should appoint two attorneys or a trust corporation to take out the grant.

8.11.6   The power of attorney can be in the general form specified in Sch. 1 to the Powers of Attorney Act 1971, in a limited form specifically intended for use in the grant application, or in the form of an enduring power of attorney under the Enduring Powers of Attorney Act 1985.

8.11.7   It should be noted that if the donor of the enduring power of attorney is incapable at the time of the application for the grant, the application should be made in accordance with section 8.6 above (r. 31(3)) and the enduring power of attorney should have been registered with the Court of Protection.

8.11.8   The power of attorney should be lodged with the application for the grant. A general power of attorney should be lodged with a copy to enable the original to be returned when the grant issues. A power of attorney limited to the grant application will be retained by the Registry.

8.11.9   If two (or more) persons entitled to a grant appoint separate attorneys, the grant may issue to the attorneys jointly.

8.12   Consular Convention grants

8.12.1   An alternative to an attorney application is possible if the application comes within the terms of the Consular Convention Act 1949.

8.12.2   In order to qualify under the Act, the person entitled to the grant must be resident out of England and Wales and a national of a state to which s. 1 of the Consular Convention Act 1949 has been applied.

8.12.3   A consular officer of the appropriate state may take out the grant on behalf of the national, as set out in section 8.12.2 above (without that person executing a power of attorney or similar document), such grant being for the use and benefit of the national until further representation is granted.

8.12.4   The oath to lead to the grant should confirm the facts in section 8.12.2 above, that the applicant is the appropriate consular officer and that s. 1 of the Consular Convention Act 1949 has been applied to the country of which the applicant is a consular officer.

8.12.5   The grant will issue to the consular officer by title (and not by name) and to his successors (Consular Convention Act 1949 s. 1(3)) and contain the same limitation as in an attorney grant (see section 8.10.1 above).

8.13   Special practice points to consider on the oath

8.13.1   The general form of oath to be applied to the case is that set out in sections 4.5 and 9.13 above.

8.13.2   It is not necessary to state whether the donor resides in or out of England and Wales.

8.13.3   The title to the grant of the donor should be set out in full as though he were applying himself.

8.13.4   The full name of the attorney should be given and he should be described as the "lawful attorney".

8.13.5   The limitation "for the use and benefit of *A.B.* and until further representation be granted" should be included after the promise to administer.
    For further details of the oath, see the precedents following paragraph 8.66 of the *Probate Manual*, 23rd edition.

8.14   Miscellaneous points

8.14.1   If the donor of a power of attorney dies during the administration of the estate, a grant of administration *de bonis non* is required.

8.14.2   Any transactions carried out by the attorney after the death of the donor are valid, provided that the attorney did not know of the donor's death (Powers of Attorney Act 1971 s. 5(1)).

8.14.3   If the attorney dies during the administration of the estate, a further grant may issue to another attorney or to the donor. This type of grant is known as a cessate grant.

8.14.4   The limitation in all grants to attorneys is "for the use and benefit of (the donors) until further representation be granted", subject to the discretion of the Registrar to issue a grant with whatever limitation he deems appropriate.
(r. 31(1))

8.14.5   It is not possible to issue a grant to an executor and the attorney of an executor for the reason that this would result in a "mixed grant" of probate and letters of administration (with will).

8.14.6   If an enduring power of attorney has been registered in the Court of Protection and the donor is not incapable, this fact should be stated in the oath when the application for the grant is made.

9. Trust Corporations, Non-Trust Corporations and Settled Land

Contents

TRUST CORPORATIONS

9.1 Introduction

9.1.1 A grant of representation may be issued to a trust corporation (Supreme Court Act 1981 s. 115(1)).

9.1.2 The grant must issue to the trust corporation by name and not to its nominee (Supreme Court Act 1981 s. 115(2)).

9.1.3 A trust corporation can be defined as a corporation (including the Public Trustee) which has been appointed by the court in any case to be a trustee or is authorised by the rules made under s. 4(3) of the Public Trustee Act 1906 to act as custodian trustee (Supreme Court Act 1981 s. 128).

9.1.4   A trust corporation may either obtain the grant on its own, or with another co-administrator (Supreme Court Act 1981 s. 114(2)).

9.2   Applications by trust corporations for a grant

9.2.1   An application for a grant to a trust corporation should be made by one of its officers swearing the oath and any other document required to lead to the grant.
(r. 36(1))

9.2.2   A trust corporation appointed executor in a will may obtain a grant of probate on its own or with any co-executor.

9.2.3   A trust corporation is deemed to be appointed executor even if only a branch office of that corporation has been appointed.

9.2.4   A trust corporation may have power reserved or renounce probate in the same manner as any other executor.

9.2.5   A renunciation by a trust corporation should either be signed by an officer of the corporation authorised to do so on its behalf or sealed with the seal of the corporation.

9.2.6   If the renunciation is signed by an officer of the corporation, a copy of the resolution authorising him so to sign should be lodged with the renunciation.

9.2.7   A trust corporation is entitled to a grant of letters of administration (with will) in the same degree as an individual under r. 20.

9.2.8   A trust corporation is most likely to be a residuary legatee and devisee in trust but some charities are entitled to act as custodian trustees if incorporated under the Charitable Trustees Incorporation Act 1872 and other bodies (such as local authorities) may also be entitled to act as custodian trustees. (Public Trustee (Custodian Trustees) Rules 1971, as amended).

9.2.9   A trust corporation may act as attorney for anyone entitled to a grant.

9.2.10   A trust corporation not named as a beneficiary in a will may take a grant of letters of administration (with will) if all the persons entitled to a grant and all persons interested in the residuary estate consent to the trust corporation acting.
(r. 36(3))

9.2.11   The Registrar has discretion to dispense with any or all of the consents referred to in section 9.2.10 above if he thinks fit.
(r. 36(3))

9.2.12   If any of the residuary beneficiaries is a minor, the persons who consent to the trust corporation taking out the grant should also renounce letters of administration (with will).

9.2.13   Grants issued in respect of section 9.2.12 above will be limited until the minor attains the age of 18 years or until further representation be granted (President's Direction 19 June 1947).

9.2.14   In the event of an intestacy, all the persons entitled to a grant may consent to a trust corporation obtaining a grant.
(r. 36(3))

9.2.15   Similarly, in a case of intestacy when some of the beneficiaries are minors, sections 9.2.12 and 9.2.13 above apply.

9.2.16   If all persons entitled to a grant of administration (with or without will) are minors, a grant may issue to a trust corporation upon the consent of the statutory, testamentary or other lawfully appointed guardian of the minors.

9.2.17   If there are no persons entitled to a grant in accordance with section 9.2.16 above, it is a matter for the Registrar's discretion as to whether the trust corporation may take the grant.

9.2.18   The grant in section 9.2.17 above will not be limited in any way (Registrar's Direction 25 February 1952).

9.2.19   The Public Trustee is entitled to a grant in the same manner as any other trust corporation.

9.2.20   The Public Trustee has the right to take *any* grant of administration (with or without will) (Public Trustee Act 1906 s. 6(1)).

9.2.21   In respect of section 9.2.20 above, the surviving spouse or next-of-kin shall be preferred to the Public Trustee in any application unless good reason is demonstrated for preference being given to the Public Trustee (Public Trustee Act 1906 s. 6(1)).

9.3 Special practice points to consider on the oath

9.3.1 The oath takes the general form set out in sections 3.2, 4.9 and 5.14 above.

9.3.2 The name of the deponent and his position in the corporation should be given in full.

9.3.3 The full name of the trust corporation and the address of its registered office should be given together with any account number which it is desired to include in the grant.

9.3.4 The usual clauses in respect of settled land, life and minority interests should be completed.

9.3.5 If the trust corporation is extracting the grant with the consents of the persons entitled thereto, the consents should be recited in the oath.

9.3.6 Details of the resolution of the trust corporation authorising the deponent to make the application on its behalf should be included, together with the fact that a certified copy thereof has been lodged with the application or that such a certified copy has been lodged with the Senior Registrar of the Family Division.
(r. 36(2)(b))

9.3.7 The fact that the corporation is a trust corporation as defined by r. 2(1) and has the power under its constitution to accept the grant applied for must be included in the oath.
(r. 36(1))

9.3.8 It is also necessary when the trust corporation is applying as executor to include a statement in the oath confirming that the usual terms and conditions of the trust corporation under which it is appointed executor in no way limits its power to act as such.

9.3.9 Any limitation (see section 9.2.13 above) should be included after the promise to administer.

For further details of the oath, see the precedent following paragraph 10.19 of the *Probate Manual*, 23rd edition.

9.4   Miscellaneous points

9.4.1   Generally speaking, corporations out of England and Wales are not
          trust corporations, but certain corporations in the Republic of Ireland
          do qualify as such if the provisions of r. 30 Public Trustee Rules
          1912, as substituted by Public Trustee (Custodian Trustee) Rules
          1971, as amended apply. The Republic's membership of the EEC
          allows these corporations to be classed as trust corporations.

9.4.2   If a minority or life interest arises, a trust corporation may take the
          grant on its own without a co-administrator, although the grant may
          issue to a trust corporation and an individual or individuals if
          required (Supreme Court Act 1981 s. 114(2)).

9.4.3   Unless the resolution authorising the deponent to act on behalf of the
          trust corporation has been filed with the Senior Registrar of the
          Family Division, a certified copy thereof should be lodged with the
          application.
          (r. 36(1)(b))

9.4.4   The certified copy resolution referred to in section 9.4.3 above is
          required in every application made by a trust corporation, whether
          or not a similar document has been lodged in a previous application
          in respect of a different estate.

9.4.5   If the trust corporation is acting with the consent of the beneficiaries,
          the original signed consents should be lodged with the application.

          CORPORATIONS OTHER THAN TRUST CORPORATIONS

9.5   Introduction

9.5.1   If a corporation is not a trust corporation ("a non-trust corporation")
          and would be entitled to a grant if it was an individual, its nominee
          may take out a grant for its use and benefit and until further
          representation be granted.
          (r. 36(4)(a))

9.5.2   The non-trust corporation may also appoint an attorney to act on its
          behalf.
          (r. 36(4)(a))

9.5.3   It should be noted that a non-trust corporation is *not* entitled to a
          grant of probate if it is appointed executor.
          (r. 36(4)(a))

9.6 Application for a grant

9.6.1   A non-trust corporation may apply for a grant by way of a nominee appointed by a resolution sealed with the corporation's seal or validated by some other means.
(r. 36(4)(b))

9.6.2   The resolution should be lodged with the papers when application is made for the grant.
(r. 36(4)(b))

9.6.3   As an alternative to nominating by way of resolution, the non-trust corporation may execute a power of attorney. This is the case whether or not the corporation has its principal place of business out of England and Wales.
(r. 36(4)(a))

9.6.4   If a non-trust corporation wishes to renounce, it may do so by way of a nominee appointed for that purpose by a resolution similar to that in section 9.6.1 above.

9.7 Special practice points to consider on the oath

9.7.1   The oath should follow the general form of oath in sections 4.9 and 5.14 above.

9.7.2   The name of the non-trust corporation should be set out in full, as should that of the person nominated to take the grant on its behalf.

9.7.3   The sections on settled land, life and minority interests should be completed.

9.7.4   If a life or minority interest arises, two applicants are required (Supreme Court Act 1981 s. 114(2)). A simple expedient to overcome this problem would be to have the non-trust corporation nominate two persons to take the grant.

9.7.5   The deponent should swear that the corporation is not a trust corporation as defined by r. 2(1).
(r. 36(4)(c))

9.7.6   The oath should contain the title to the grant of the non-trust corporation under the terms of the will and details of the resolution or power of attorney authorising the deponent to take the grant.

9.7.7   The limitation "for the use and benefit of (the non-trust corporation)
        and until further representation be granted" should be included
        after the promise to administer.

9.8   Miscellaneous points

9.8.1   If a non-trust corporation is entitled to a grant solely as executor, a
        copy of its constitution should be lodged to show that it is entitled to
        apply for a grant thereby (Registrar's Direction, 2 January 1956).

9.8.2   It is not possible for a non-trust corporation and an individual where
        both have been appointed executors to make a joint application for a
        grant.
        (r. 36(4)(d))

9.8.3   If a non-trust corporation is appointed executor together with an
        individual, upon the renunciation of the individual the nominee of
        the non-trust corporation may take the grant as set out in section 9.6
        above.

9.8.4   As an alternative to section 9.8.3 above, the individual executor
        appointed with a non-trust corporation may apply for a grant of
        probate alone if it is sworn in the oath that the corporation is not a
        trust corporation.

9.8.5   If it is desired, a grant may issue to the attorney of an individual
        executor and of a non-trust corporation appointed executor.
        (r. 31(1), 36(4)(a))

SETTLED LAND

9.9   Introduction

9.9.1   Settled land is governed by the Settled Land Act 1925.

9.9.2   "Settled land" can be defined as land in which the beneficial owner
        has a limited or qualified interest (Settled Land Act 1925 s. 2).

9.9.3   Settled land includes any type of immovable property, including
        such property as has been purchased with the proceeds of sale of
        settled land.

9.9.4   Settlements of land may be made either by a deed executed in the lifetime of the settlor or by a will.

9.9.5   To be settled land, the property must have been vested in the tenant for life by the trustees appointed thereto.

9.9.6   The ultimate beneficiary of the property is known as "the remainderman".

9.9.7   Settled land does not include land in respect of which there is an immediate binding trust for sale, whether or not the power to sell is deferred or is subject to the consent of any person (Settled Land Act 1925 s. 1(7)).

9.9.8   Land usually ceases to be settled land on the death of the last tenant for life.

9.10   Application for a grant in respect of settled land

9.10.1   A grant limited to settled land or including settled land may be made.

9.10.2   The persons entitled to apply for a settled land grant are as follows:
   (a) the special executors as constituted by s. 22 of the Administration of Estates Act 1925 have the prior right to a grant of probate limited to settled land (r. 29(2));
   (b) the trustees of the settlement at the time of the application for the grant (r. 29(3)(i));
   (c) the personal representatives of the tenant for life (r. 29(3)(ii)).

9.10.3   If the persons entitled to apply for a grant in respect of the free estate are also entitled to a grant in respect of settled land, a grant "including settled land" may issue.
   (r. 29(4))

9.10.4   If a grant to the free estate only is made, it must be worded so as to exclude settled land.
   (r. 29(5)).

9.10.5   If the will has not been proved before the application for the settled land grant is made, its validity should be established in the usual way and it should be marked by the applicants and Commissioner in accordance with r. 10.

9.10.6   If the will has already been proved and a grant "save and except settled land" issued, it is not necessary for the will to be marked by the applicants and swearing Commissioner. However, a copy of the will is annexed to the grant.

9.10.7   "Special executors" in section 9.10.2(a) above are the persons who were the trustees of the settlement at the date of death of the deceased (testate) tenant for life (Administration of Estates Act 1925 s. 22).

9.10.8   Special executors are entitled before anyone else to a grant limited to settled land and are the only persons entitled to a grant of probate thereto.

9.10.9   A grant in section 9.10.8 above may be issued before or after a general grant.

9.10.10   It should be noted that a chain of executorship cannot pass through a special executor (Registrar's Direction 21 July 1936).

9.10.11   If there are no trustees of the settlement surviving at the date of death of the deceased tenant for life, the trustees subsequently appointed are entitled to a grant of letters of administration (with or without will).
          (r. 29(3)(i))

9.10.12   If there is one trustee surviving who was a trustee at the date of death of the (testate) tenant for life and a trustee or trustees have been appointed subsequently, the former is entitled to a grant of probate limited to settled land alone as special executor to the exclusion of the latter.

9.10.13   In the case of section 9.10.12 above, if the special executor renounces probate he may still join with the other trustees in an application for letters of administration (with or without will) limited to settled land in accordance with r. 29(3)(i).
          (r. 37(1))

9.10.14   If there are no persons in sections 9.10.8 and 9.10.11 above, the personal representative of the tenant for life may take the grant.
          (r. 29(3)(ii))

9.10.15   In cases where the persons entitled to the settled land grant are also entitled to a grant in respect of the free estate, a grant "including settled land" may issue to them.
          (r. 29(4))

9.10.16 It should be noted that in the event that a trustee (whether appointed before or after the date of death of the deceased) survives, it is not possible for a grant to be made in accordance with section 9.10.14 above.

9.10.17 In section 9.10.11 above, the term "trustees" includes the personal representative of the person who set up the settlement ("the settlor") in the event that there are no other trustees and the settlement arose under a will or intestacy (Settled Land Act 1925 s. 30(3)).

9.10.18 In the event of there being no-one in section 9.10.2 above able or willing to apply for a grant, the Registrar has discretion to make an order in favour of the remainderman or a person interested in the settled land under s. 116 of the Supreme Court Act 1981.

9.11 Special practice points to consider on the oath – grant "limited to settled land"

9.11.1 The oath in applications for a grant limited to settled land follows the general form in sections 3.2, 4.9 and 5.4 above.

9.11.2 Only one applicant is required even if a life or minority interest arises in respect of the land. This is because the interest arises under the settlement and not out of the estate.

9.11.3 The marking of the will under r. 10 applies to section 9.10.5 above.

9.11.4 Care should be taken to ensure that the oath states that there was land vested in the deceased which was settled previously to his death and which remained settled land notwithstanding his death.

9.11.5 Details of any former grant should be recited in the oath and an office copy of that grant should be lodged with the papers.

9.11.6 Details of the settlement should be recited in the oath. If the settlement was made by a testamentary document, the full name of the testator, the date the testamentary document was proved and the Registry at which it was proved should be included in the oath. If the settlement was made by a deed, the date should be included.

9.11.7 The words "limited to the said settled land" should be included after the words "gross value of the said estate".

9.12   Special practice points to consider on the oath: grant "save and except settled land"

9.12.1   Sections 9.11.1 and 9.11.4 to 9.11.6 above all apply to oaths in support of applications for grants "save and except settled land".

9.12.2   If the will has already been proved, the applicants and Commissioner should mark (in accordance with r. 10) an office copy thereof. This should be stated in the oath.

9.12.3   No details of the settlement need to be recited in the oath.

9.12.4   The words "save and except settled land" should be included after the words "gross value of the said estate".

9.13   Special practice points to consider on the oath: grant "including settled land"

9.13.1   Sections 9.11.1, 9.11.4 and 9.11.6 above all apply to oaths in support of applications for grants "including settled land".

9.13.2   The words "including settled land" should be added after the words "gross value of the said estate".

9.13.3   The value of the settled land should be included in the total gross and net estates and should also be shown as a separate figure after the net estate.

      For further details of the oaths see the precedents following paragraph 10.42 of the *Probate Manual*, 23rd edition.

9.14   Miscellaneous points

9.14.1   If it is desired to obtain a grant limited to settled land, any previous grant issued in the estate should specifically exclude settled land. If the previous grant was not one "save and except settled land", it should be amended (see Chapter 13 for further details on amending grants).

9.14.2   If there is more than one tenant for life, these joint tenants constitute the tenant for life. The death of the first joint tenant in such circumstances extinguishes his rights in the settled land.

9.14.3   When an application is made in respect of a deceased in whom settled land was vested at the date of his death, all the deeds, settlements and vesting documents should be lodged when the application is made.

9.14.4   It is advisable to seek guidance of the Registrar before making the application for grant if there is any complication in the case.

9.14.5   It should be noted that the special executor has the right to renounce probate or have power reserved to him in the same manner (and with the same restrictions) as a general executor.

9.14.6   The appropriate form of Inland Revenue account is required. This is governed by the type of grant needed. For further details, see section 6.4. above.

9.14.7   Where settled land arises, there can be no question of the estate being treated as an excepted estate.

9.14.8   No fees are payable in respect of settled land but in the event that the grant is limited to settled land a court fee of £2.00 is payable. If a grant including settled land is required, the value of the settled land should be deducted from the net estate to calculate the figure upon which court fees are payable.

10. De Bonis Non, Cessate Grants, Grants Limited to Part of the Estate and Discretionary Grant Applications

Contents

APPLICATIONS DE BONIS NON ADMINISTRATIS

10.1 Introduction

10.1.1 If the executors or administrators who have taken the grant die with out completing the administration of the estate and there is no cha of executorship, a grant of administration *de bonis non administratis* (of the unadministered estate) may issue.

10.1.2 A grant *de bonis non* can only be issued if there is estate remaining unadministered.

10.1.3 A grant *de bonis non* is always of administration (with or without will annexed).

10.1.4 If possible, the application for the grant of administration *de bonis non* should be made by someone of equal title with the previous administrator.

10.1.5 A person in section 10.1.4 above will be preferred to someone who is the legal personal representative of a person with equal title unless the Registrar otherwise directs.
(r. 27(5))

10.2 Grants of administration (with will) de bonis non

10.2.1 If the sole or surviving proving executor dies leaving part of the estate unadministered, a further grant is required to deal with the remaining assets.

10.2.2 A *de bonis non* grant cannot issue until all the executors appointed by the will (including executors to whom power has been reserved) have been cleared off.

10.2.3 If a chain of executorship arises (see section 3.4.4 above), a grant *de bonis non* cannot issue, as the unadministered estate can be dealt with by the deceased executor's executor.

10.2.4 A chain of executorship is said to be in abeyance if the sole or surviving proving executor dies leaving a will appointing executors who neither prove the will nor renounce probate.

10.2.5 In the circumstances of section 10.2.4 above, a grant *de bonis non* may issue limited until the executor proves the deceased executor's will.

10.2.6 Once the executors (and any residuary legatee or devisee holding in trust for another person) have been cleared off, a grant *de bonis non* may issue to any residuary beneficiary named in the will or to the person entitled to the undisposed of estate.

10.2.7   In the event that the persons in section 10.2.6 above renounce letters
         of administration (with will), the grant may issue to those persons
         entitled in the order of priority in r. 20.

10.2.8   If the person entitled to a grant *de bonis non* in sections 10.2.6 and
         10.2.7 above has died, a grant in respect of his estate is necessary so
         that a personal representative of that person is constituted before a *de*
         bonis non grant can issue. This grant is called the "leading grant".

10.2.9   Unless a chain of executorship exists in respect of the leading grant,
         a grant to the estate of the person entitled to the *de bonis non* grant is
         always required, save in the circumstances set out in section
         10.13.2(e) below.

10.3   Special practice points to consider in the oath – grant of administration (with will) de bonis non

10.3.1   The oath follows the general form of oath as set out in section 4.
         above.

10.3.2   An office copy of the deceased's will should be marked by the appli
         cants and the swearing commissioner in accordance with r. 10. The
         will should be described as an "office copy" in the oath.

10.3.3   Details of the former grant (date and place of issue) and the fact tha
         the administrator has died leaving part of the estate unadministere
         should be recited. Similar details in respect of any leading grant
         should be included.

10.3.4   It should be shown that any possible chain of executorship has bee
         broken (e.g. "that on the ...... day of .... 19... probate
         the will of the said deceased was granted out of the Wincheste
         District Probate Registry of this Division to *A.B.*, the sole execute
         named in the said will, who died on the ...... day of ......
         19... *intestate* leaving part of the estate unadministered").

10.3.5   The clearing required to establish the applicant's title should
         included as well as details of any leading grant.

10.3.6   The estate should be described as "unadministered" and only a gro
         figure should be shown.

10.3.7   It is possible for a *de bonis non* application to be treated as an excepted estate (see section 6.3 above). In these circumstances, only the gross figure should be shown.

10.4   Grants of letters of administration de bonis non

10.4.1   The grant of letters of administration *de bonis non* should issue to someone of equal title to the grant with the deceased grantee. If there is no-one of equal title with the grantee or those persons have renounced, or the Registrar has otherwise directed (r. 27(5)), the *de bonis non* grant may issue to the legal personal representative of someone who had equal title with the previous grantee.

10.4.2   Section 10.4.1 above does not apply in the case in which the surviving spouse was one of the persons entitled to share in the estate. In such cases, the legal personal representative of the spouse has a prior right to the grant over any other legal personal representative of a person entitled to the grant (see r. 22(4)).

10.4.3   The value of the unadministered estate may determine the person who may apply for a grant *de bonis non.*

10.4.4   The estate remaining unadministered should be valued at the date of application and if the estate has increased in value (either by an increase in value of the known assets or by the discovery of further estate since the issue of the original grant), it may be that the value of the unadministered estate now exceeds the value of the estate shown in the original grant.

10.4.5   If the original grant was to the surviving spouse and the circumstances in section 10.4.4 above apply, in the event that the statutory legacy in force at the date of death is exceeded, the deceased's next of kin may be entitled as of right to apply for a grant.

10.4.6   An example of the situation in section 10.4.5 above is the case in which the surviving spouse was entitled to extract the original grant alone but the value of the unadministered estate now exceeds the surviving spouse's statutory legacy in force at the date of death of the deceased. In these circumstances, any children of the deceased are now entitled to share in the estate and have a prior title to the grant over the legal personal representative of the spouse. In the absence of any children, those persons entitled to a share in the estate (see section 5.3.2 above) also have a prior title to the grant over the legal personal representative of the spouse.

10.5   Special practice points to consider on the oath – grants of letters of administration de bonis non

10.5.1   The oath follows the general form of oath set out in section 5.13 above.

10.5.2   Sections 10.3.3 and 10.3.5 to 10.3.7 above apply to grants of letters of administration *de bonis non*.

For further details about the oaths in sections 10.3 and 10.5 above, see the precedents following paragraph 11.10 of the *Probate Manual*, 23rd edition.

10.6   Miscellaneous points

10.6.1   The death of the donor of a power of attorney during the administration of the estate requires the issue of a grant *de bonis non* to enable the administration of the estate to continue.

10.6.2   It is sometimes necessary to issue a grant *de bonis non* in respect of a nil estate. In these circumstances, the reason for requiring the grant should be included in the oath.

10.6.3   If an Inland Revenue account is required, it should be in form A-5C and sworn by the applicant if the date of death is before 13 March 1975. The account (or affidavit) must be controlled (i.e. certified and stamped by the Capital Taxes Office) before the grant can issue.

10.6.4   It should be noted that two applicants are required if a life or minority interest arises unless the Registrar otherwise directs or a trust corporation obtains the grant. (Supreme Court Act 1981 s. 114(2)).

10.6.5   The fee payable on a *de bonis non* application is £2.00, regardless of the value of the unadministered estate.

CESSATE GRANTS

10.7   Introduction

10.7.1   A cessate grant issues if the previous limited grant is no longer operative by virtue of it having ceased to be effective by some contingency recited in the grant or by some other happening.

10.7.2   Examples covered by section 10.7.1 above include cases in which the limitation has become operative (a minor having attained 18 years of age, the donor of a power of attorney making application for a grant), or an executor for life having died after proving the will.

10.7.3   A cessate grant is a full grant of the whole of the estate: this is the difference between a cessate and *de bonis non* grant, as the latter is a grant only of the unadministered estate.

10.8   Persons entitled to apply for a cessate grant

10.8.1   Generally speaking, a cessate grant issues to the person for whose use and benefit the previous limited grant was issued.

10.8.2   An exception to section 10.8.1 above is the case of the death of an attorney or the administrator on behalf of a mentally incapable person.

10.8.3   In the event of the occurrence of the first circumstance in section 10.8.2 above, a further attorney can be appointed by the person entitled to the grant and on the occurrence of the second, the provision of r. 35 applied to constitute a new administrator.

10.9   Special practice points to consider on the oath

10.9.1   The oath follows the same general form as that for a *de bonis non* application (see sections 10.3 and 10.5 above).

10.9.2   As well as including details of the former grant, the oath should contain the reasons for the cessation of the former grant.

10.9.3   Although the grant is issued in respect of the whole of the estate, the figure shown on the oath is the unadministered estate and should be described as such.

For further details of the oath, see the precedents following paragraph 11.16 of the *Probate Manual*, 23rd edition.

GRANTS LIMITED TO PART OF THE ESTATE

10.10   Introduction

10.10.1 The court has power to grant probate or administration of any part of the estate of the deceased limited in whatever manner the court wishes (Supreme Court Act 1981 s. 113(1)).

10.10.2 The power in section 10.10.1 above is limited to dealing only with trust property if the estate is insolvent (Supreme Court Act 1981 s. 113(2)).

10.11   Application for the grant

10.11.1 If a grant in section 10.10.1 above is required, the application should be made to the Registrar for an order under s. 113 of the Supreme Court Act 1981.

10.11.2 The application in section 10.11.1 above is made on an ex-parte basis, supported by an affidavit of facts, which should set out the reasons for the application and:
  (a) confirm whether the estate of the deceased is insolvent
  (b) show how any person entitled to a full grant in priority to the applicant has been cleared off (r. 51).

10.11.3 It should be noted that an order under s. 113 of the Supreme Court Act 1981 is required whether or not the applicant is entitled to a full grant as of right.

10.11.4 The oath should be in the general form applicable to the type of grant.

10.11.5 The usual rules apply in respect of life and minority interests.

10.11.6 Details of the Registrar's Order should be included in the oath: no other clearing is required.

10.11.7 Only the value of the property in respect of which the grant is sought should be shown on the oath.

10.12   Miscellaneous points

10.12.1 A grant in section 10.10 above may be an "excepted estate". If it is not, the appropriate Inland Revenue account should be filed (see section 6.4 above).

10.12.2 The fee for an application for a grant under s. 113 is calculated as for a normal full grant.

DISCRETIONARY GRANTS

10.13 Section 116 Supreme Court Act 1981 – introduction

10.13.1 The court has power to grant administration (with or without will) to whomsoever it chooses and with whatever limitation is deemed suitable (Supreme Court Act 1981 s. 116).

10.13.2 Examples of the court exercising the power in section 10.13.1 above are:
(a) the persons entitled to a grant under the rules are missing or considered unsuitable to administer the estate;
(b) as a compromise in a dispute between persons equally entitled to a grant (such as executors);
(c) in order to assist in the commencement or continuation of an action;
(d) when the person entitled to the grant has been found guilty of the murder or manslaughter of the deceased;
(e) to obviate the necessity of obtaining a leading grant (see sections 10.1ff above);
(f) to pass over an executor who has intermeddled in the estate and who has been cited to take a grant but has not done so (see section 14.6 below).
There are many other types of application in which s. 116 of the Supreme Court Act 1981 may apply.

10.13.3 It should be noted that the Registrar has power to direct that the applicants for an order issue a summons returnable before himself and served upon those persons whom it is sought to pass over.

10.14 Application for the grant

10.14.1 An application for an order under s. 116 of the Supreme Court Act 1981 is made on an ex-parte basis to the Registrar of the Registry out of which it is desired to extract the grant, supported by an affidavit of facts setting out the grounds of the application.
(r. 52(a))

10.14.2 Details of the order should be recited in the oath to lead to the grant.

10.14.3 A life or minority interest arising in the estate is subject to the same general rule as in any ordinary application (Supreme Court Act 1981 s. 114(2)).

10.14.4 If a life or minority interest arises and two applicants are required, the Registrar will appoint two persons to take the grant in his order.

10.14.5 It should be noted that no clearing is necessary on the oath and the applicant's title to the grant arises solely out of the order.

10.15   Discretionary grants ad colligenda bona – introduction

10.15.1 If the estate is in danger of suffering loss by a delay in constituting an administrator and it is not possible to take out a full grant as quickly as desired, the court has power to issue a limited grant to safeguard the estate.

10.15.2 The order will normally be limited "for the purpose only of collecting and getting in and receiving the estate and doing such acts as may be necessary for the preservation of the same and until further representation be granted", although the Registrar may direct some variation or other form of limitation if appropriate.

10.15.3 The grant is always of administration. If the deceased left a will, it is not proved and no reference is made to it either on the oath or grant. The grant will not state whether or not the deceased died intestate.

10.15.4 The Registrar has similar discretionary powers to choose the administrator as he has in applications under s. 116 of the Supreme Court Act 1981 (see section 10.13 above).

10.16   Application for the grant

10.16.1 The application for an order for a grant of letters of administration *ad colligenda bona* is made on an ex-parte basis to the Registrar supported by an affidavit setting out the grounds of the application, including the reason for the urgency.
(r. 52(b))

10.16.2 The oath follows the general form for administrators and if a life or minority interest arises, the usual considerations apply (Supreme Court Act 1981, s. 114(2))

10.16.3 Details of the order should appear on the oath, and the limitation (see section 10.15.2 above) should appear after the promise to administer.

10.16.4 Section 10.14.5 above applies equally to cases of administration *ad colligenda bona*.

10.17 Discretionary grant for administration pending suit: introduction

10.17.1 If proceedings are pending in respect of the validity of a will or to obtain, recall or revoke a grant and it is necessary to obtain a grant as a matter of urgency, the court may appoint an administrator to act whilst the action is continuing (Supreme Court Act 1981, s. 117(1)).

10.17.2 The administrator has all the powers of a general administrator subject to the court having control of and the power to direct the estate's administration (Supreme Court Act 1981, s. 117(2)).

10.17.3 Unless the court directs otherwise, no distribution of the estate can take place under a grant of administration pending suit (Supreme Court Act 1981, s. 117(2)).

10.17.4 The court has power to order such remuneration as it thinks fit to be paid out of the estate to the administrator (Supreme Court Act 1981, s. 117(3)).

10.17.5 Generally speaking, a party to the action obtains the grant, although the court can direct the application for the grant to be made by whomsoever it considers appropriate.

10.17.6 A grant of administration pending suit is of administration only. If the deceased left a will, it is not proved.

10.18 Application for a grant of administration pending suit

10.18.1 The order to lead to the grant is made by a Master of the Chancery Division by way of summons.

10.18.2 The oath to lead to the grant follows the general form of an administration oath.

10.18.3 The grant may be made to a single administrator notwithstanding the existence of a life or minority interest (*re Haslip* [1958] 2 All ER 275). However, the oath should still state whether such an interest arises.
(r. 8(4))

10.18.4 Full details of the order should be given in the oath, including the limitation which should appear after the promise to administer.

10.18.5 When the application for the grant is made an office copy of the order should be lodged together with the oath and Inland Revenue account (if required).

10.19   Miscellaneous points

10.19.1 A grant of administration pending suit can only issue from the Principal Registry.

10.19.2 At the end of the action, the grant of administration pending suit ceases and a full grant is required.

10.19.3 Application for the full grant can be made at any registry or sub-registry.

10.19.4 The oath to lead to the full grant should contain details of the final order and of the former grant.

10.19.5 An office copy of the final order should be lodged with the application for the full grant.

11. Commorientes, Leave to Swear Death, Murder and Manslaughter

Contents

COMMORIENTES

11.1 Introduction

11.1.1 On those occasions when two or more persons die in circumstances rendering it uncertain who survived the other or others, the devolution of their estates is consequently uncertain.

11.1.2 The general rule is that in the circumstances of section 11.1.1 above, the younger of the deceased persons is deemed to have survived the elder (Law of Property Act 1925 s. 184)).

11.1.3 Section 11.1.2 above may not apply in the event that one or more of the persons has executed a will making an effective disposition of his estate.

11.1.4 Section 11.1.2 above is amended in the case of a husband and wife dying in circumstances rendering it uncertain who survived the other on or after 1 January 1953 (Intestates Estates Act 1952).

PN—G

11.1.5   In the event that a husband and wife die in circumstances rendering it uncertain who survived the other, if either of the spouses died wholly intestate the rule in section 11.1.2 above does not apply and it is deemed that the estate of the spouse who died intestate passes as if the other spouse did not survive.

11.1.6   Section 11.1.5 above applies in respect of any undisposed of estate under the terms of a will (Administration of Estates Act 1925 (as amended) s. 46(3)).

11.2   Application for the grant

11.2.1   If there is uncertainty as to survivorship, evidence must be supplied to satisfy the Registrar that the two or more deceased died in circumstances rendering it uncertain who survived the other.

11.2.2   The evidence in section 11.2.1 above may take the form of an affidavit by the person who found the bodies or the doctor who performed the post-mortem. Additional evidence (such as evidence before the Coroner's Court) should also be lodged if available.

11.2.3   Reference should be made to the Registrar with the evidence as soon as it is available to enable him to decide whether the case can proceed on the basis that uncertainty of survivorship arises.

11.2.4   Once the Registrar has made his ruling, the application proceeds in the same manner as an ordinary application for letters of administration (with or without will). It should be noted that there is no Registrar's Order made in these cases.

11.3   Special practice points to consider on the oath

11.3.1   The oath follows the same general form as that set out in sections 4.9 and 5.13 above.

11.3.2   The question of a life or minority interest must be dealt with as in an ordinary application and the same considerations apply as to the number of applicants required.

11.3.3   The oath should state that: "all possible enquiries have been made and it appears that A. and B. died in circumstances rendering it uncertain who survived the other".

11.3.4   Where appropriate, the presumption under s. 184 of the Law of Property Act 1925 (e.g. "that by virtue of s. 184 of the Law of Property Act 1925, the said *A.* is (by virtue of being the younger) deemed to have survived the said *B.*") should be included.

11.3.5   In the event that sections 11.1.4 to 11.1.6 apply, there is no need to include section 11.3.4 in the oath.
   For the form of the oath, see the precedents following paragraph 12.09 of the *Probate Manual*, 23rd edition.

11.4   Miscellaneous points

11.4.1   It should be noted that no title to the grant can pass through the estate of a deceased minor in whom the estate did not vest and any application for a *commorientes* grant should take this into account (Administration of Estates Act 1925 (as amended) s. 47(2)).

11.4.2   In the case of persons dying domiciled abroad and in circumstances rendering it uncertain who survived the other, the law of the domicile applies and not the practice as set out above.

LEAVE TO SWEAR DEATH

11.5   Introduction

11.5.1   In the event that the death of the deceased cannot be proved, it is open to the applicant to apply for an order of the Registrar giving leave for death to be sworn as having occurred on or since a certain date.
   (r. 53)

11.5.2   It should be noted that this application is for leave to swear death *in probate proceedings*. It is *not* proof of death or a presumption of death. It cannot be used as a basis of a petition of dissolution or nullity of marriage.

11.6   Application for the order

11.6.1   An application for leave to swear death is made to the Registrar on an ex-parte basis, supported by an affidavit of facts.
   (r. 53)

11.6.2   The affidavit should set out the grounds of the application and should
         list any insurance policies on the life of the person who is the subject
         of the application, together with any supporting evidence the
         Registrar may require.
         (r. 53)

11.6.3   The fullest possible evidence should be provided and should include
         (1) the last known whereabouts of the presumed deceased;
         (2) if the presumed deceased was last known to have been on board a
              boat or aircraft, what evidence is available to show that he was
              actually on board at the appropriate time;
         (3) if the presumed deceased was insured, whether notice has been
              given to the insurance companies and the nature of their replies.
              It should be noted that the Registrar will require notice to be
              given to the insurance companies before he will make the order;
         (4) evidence of the last communications from the presumed deceased
         (5) the value of the estate;
         (6) the date on or since which the death is presumed to have
              occurred.
         The list above is not exhaustive and the Registrar may well require
         other facts to be covered in the particular circumstances of an
         application.

11.6.4   Whenever possible, affidavits supporting that of the applicant should
         be lodged.

11.6.5   Once the order has been made, it is retained in the Registry and is
         not handed out, neither will a copy be supplied.

11.6.6   Details of the order may be noted from the original for inclusion in
         the oath.

11.7   Special practice points to consider on the oath

11.7.1   The oath follows the same general form as in sections 3.2, 4.9 and
         5.14 above.

11.7.2   Life and minority interests are dealt with in the same manner as in a
         normal application.

11.7.3   Death should be sworn as having occurred "on or since" a certain
         date.

11.7.4   Details of the order should be recited in the oath.

MURDER AND MANSLAUGHTER

11.8 Introduction

11.8.1 It is against public policy for a person who unlawfully kills another to benefit from that person's estate.

11.8.2 This applies to cases of murder and manslaughter (including cases of diminished responsibility).

11.8.3 An exception to section 11.8.1 above applies in cases in which a successful application is made under the Forfeiture Act 1982 to modify the forfeiture rule.

11.8.4 The Forfeiture Act 1982 permits the court to modify the effect of the forfeiture rule (s. 2).

11.8.5 If the court is satisfied under all the circumstances that the forfeiture rule should be modified, it may do so, but the modification may be in respect of only part of the property.

11.8.6 Application under the Act should be made within three months of the date of conviction.

11.8.7 It is possible to make an application under the Forfeiture Act 1982 if the killing took place before 13 October 1982.

11.8.8 Section 11.8.4 above does not apply if the conviction is for murder (Forfeiture Act 1982 s. 5).

11.9 Application for the grant

11.9.1 The application for the grant is by way of an order under s. 116 of the Supreme Court Act 1981. This should be made in accordance with section 10.13ff above.

11.9.2 The certificate of conviction should be exhibited to the affidavit of facts and a statement that no application under the Forfeiture Act 1982 has been made should be included.

11.10 Special practice points to consider on the oath

11.10.1 The oath follows the same general form as sections 4.9 and 5.14 above.

11.10.2 Sections 10.14.3 to 10.14.5 above apply in respect of these applications.

11.11   Miscellaneous points

11.11.1 It has been decided that the forfeited share of the deceased's estate passes to the other beneficiaries and not to the Crown (*re Callaway, Callaway v Treasury Solicitor* [1956] 2 All ER 451).

11.11.2 Section 11.11.1 above applies in cases of class gifts in that the forfeited share passes to the other members of the class.

12. Resealing

Contents

12.1   Resealing – introduction

12.1.1   In certain cases, it is possible to reseal a grant of representation issued by a foreign court (Colonial Probates Acts 1892 and 1927).

12.1.2   There are advantages in resealing the grant (ease of application, minimum of documentation), but it must be remembered that the name of the person who obtains the reseal will not appear on any of the documents issued by the court and a further document (such as a power of attorney) will probably be required.

12.1.3   Grants issued in Scotland and Northern Ireland cannot be resealed (Administration of Estates Act 1971 s. 1(1)).

12.1.4   Scottish confirmations and grants of representation issued in Northern Ireland in respect of persons domiciled in these countries can be used for estates in England and Wales without any further formalities (Administration of Estates Act 1971 s. 1(2) and (4)).

12.1.5   Similar reciprocal provisions for recognising grants in Scotland and Northern Ireland exist in respect of English grants of representation of persons domiciled in England and Wales (Administration of Estates Act 1971 ss. 2 and 3).

12.2   Application for resealing

12.2.1   Only grants issued by countries to which the Colonial Probates Acts 1892 and 1927 have been applied can be resealed.

12.2.2   The territories to which the Acts apply are:
          Aden (but see section 12.2.3 below)
          Alberta
          Antigua
          Australian Capital Territory
          Bahamas
          Barbados
          Belize (formerly British Honduras)
          Bermuda
          Botswana (formerly Bechuanaland)
          British Antarctic Territory
          British Columbia
          British Sovereign Base Areas in Cyprus
          Brunei
          Cayman Islands
          Christmas Island (Australian)
          Cocos (Keeling) Islands
          Cyprus (Republic)
          Dominica
          Falkland Islands
          Falkland Islands Dependencies
          Fiji
          Gambia
          Ghana
          Gibraltar
          Gilbert and Ellis Islands
          Grenada
          Guyana (formerly British Guiana)
          Hong Kong
          Jamaica
          Kenya
          Kiribati
          Lesotho (formerly Basutoland)
          Malawi
          Malaysia
          Manitoba
          Montserrat
          New Brunswick
          New Guinea Territory
          New Hebrides (except grants issued on or after 30 July 1980)
          New South Wales
          New Zealand
          Newfoundland
          Nigeria
          Norfolk Island

Northern Territory of Australia
North-West Territories of Canada
Nova Scotia
Ontario
Papua New Guinea
Prince Edward Island
Queensland
St. Christopher (St. Kitts), Nevis and Anguilla
St. Helena
St. Lucia
St. Vincent
Saskatchewan
Seychelles
Sierra Leone
Singapore
Solomon Islands
South Africa
South Australia
Southern Rhodesia (now Zimbabwe)
Sri Lanka (formerly Ceylon)
Swaziland
Tanzania
Tasmania
Tortola (formerly Virgin Islands)
Trinidad and Tobago
Turks and Caicos Islands
Tuvalu (formerly Ellice Islands)
Uganda
Victoria
Western Australia
Zambia
Zimbabwe (formerly Southern Rhodesia)

12.2.3   It should be noted that on 13 November 1967 Aden ceased to be a territory to which the Colonial Probates Acts 1892 and 1927 applied. Consequently, grants made after that date cannot be resealed (Secretary's Circular 17 January 1968).

12.2.4   The grant to be resealed will normally be accepted without question if:
   (a) it was issued by the court of domicile, or
   (b) it was issued to the person entrusted with the administration of the estate by the court of the deceased's domicile, or

(c) it was issued to the person beneficially entitled to the deceased's estate by the law of the place where the deceased died domiciled, or

(d) the will is in English or Welsh and has been proved by the executor named therein or by the executor according to the tenor of the will and is admissible to proof in England and Wales (r. 39(3)).

12.2.5   Evidence in respect of the applicant's title as in section 12.2.4 above should take the form of the grant issued by the court of domicile or an affidavit of law in the absence of such a grant.

12.2.6   If the application does not fall within the ambit of section 12.2.4 above, leave of the Registrar is required before the grant can be resealed.
(r. 39(3))

12.2.7   No limited or temporary grant can be resealed without leave of the Registrar.
(r. 39(4))

12.2.8   The exception to section 12.2.7 above is a grant in relation to personal estate only when no leave to reseal is required (Registrar's Direction, 26 May 1936).

12.2.9   Grants in respect of a nil estate in England and Wales can be resealed if a reason for requiring the reseal is given (President's Direction, 4 March 1942). (cf. section 7.7.10 above.)

12.2.10 It is possible for a grant to be resealed on more than one occasion in the event that a further grantee has been added to the original grant by the court which issued it.

12.2.11 In the event that a grant of probate and double probate has issued, both grants will be resealed if they are bound together in the same document (or presented for resealing together) and all the surviving grantees apply for the reseal.

12.2.12 Duplicate grants may be resealed without any explanation as to why such a document is required (Registrar's Direction, 18 July 1941).

12.2.13 Documents issued as a grant may be resealed, as may be the following:
(a) an exemplification of the grant (a document which contains all the essential parts of the grant and a copy of the will);

(b) an election to administer, provided it is certified on behalf of the trustee company to whom the election was issued that it is still in force and an undertaking given that in the event that the election becomes ineffective in the country of issue no further steps will be taken in the administration of the estate in England and Wales until a grant has been extracted in the country of issue;

(c) similar documents to (b) above.

12.3 Procedure on an application for resealing

12.3.1 Application for resealing may be made at any district probate registry or sub-registry or at the Principal Registry.

12.3.2 The application may be made by all the grantees or by someone with the written authority of the grantees (see section 12.4.7 below).

12.3.3 The authorisation referred to in section 12.3.2 above may take the form of a letter of authority appointing a named person or persons to apply for a reseal or a power of attorney specifically authorising the donees to apply for a reseal.

12.3.4 The application can be made by a solicitor or by the grantee (or the person authorised by him) by post. In the latter case, the application may be made by the person authorised by the grantee to the personal application section of any registry or sub-registry. An application may be made by post from outside England and Wales.

12.3.5 The documents required on a reseal application are:

(a) the original grant or a duplicate issued and sealed by the court of issue or a copy thereof certified by the court of issue, or an exemplification of the same;

(b) a copy of the grant for retention by the Registry on resealing;

(c) a copy of the will certified as accurate by the court which issued the original grant together with a copy for filing (r. 39(5));

(d) the power of attorney or letter of authority authorising the applicant to reseal the grant;

(e) the appropriate Inland Revenue account duly controlled by the Capital Taxes Office (see section 6.4.5 above) (r. 39(2)).

12.4 Miscellaneous points

12.4.1 No oath is required on an application for resealing.

12.4.2 A chain of executorship can pass through a Colonial grant but only if all the relevant grants have been resealed in England and Wales.

12.4.3   It should be noted that the court is not obliged to reseal a Colonial grant, even if the Colonial Probates Act 1892 and 1927 apply, if there are doubts about the suitability of the grant (Colonial Probates Act 1892, s. 2). Examples are given in sections 12.4.4 to 12.4.6 below.

12.4.4   Only a grant which was originally issued in English can be resealed. A grant issued in a foreign language will not be resealed, even if it is accompanied by a translation.

12.4.5   If the Colonial grant contains more than four grantees, all of whom are alive at the time the application to reseal is made, it is doubtful whether the grant should be resealed.

12.4.6   Difficulties in resealing may arise if the country in which the grant issues is subject to occupation by a foreign army and an imposed system of law.

12.4.7   All the surviving grantees on the Colonial grant should either join in the application for resealing or consent to the grant being resealed on the application of those grantees wishing to obtain the reseal.

12.4.8   It is the practice of the registries to place the seal of the court on the office copy grant issued by the foreign court. No separate document confirming this is produced and no copy of the resealed document is issued. If office copies are required, a document recording the facts of the original grant is supplied.

13. Amendment, Notation, Revocation and Duplicate Grants

Contents

AMENDMENT OF GRANT

13.1 Introduction

13.1.1 If a grant has issued containing an error, the Registrar may allow the grant to be amended.

13.1.2 If the error in the grant has been made by the court, the grant will be re-issued in the correct form by the issuing registry, if it is returned within fourteen days of issue and has not been registered.

13.1.3 If such a grant as in 13.1.2 above has been registered or is returned after the expiration of fourteen days, the Registrar will make an order for amendment. No affidavit will normally be required.

13.1.4 When making an application for amendment, all sealed copies of the grant should be returned to the Registry, together with the original.

13.1.5 It should be noted that no unofficial amendment to the grant should be made.

13.2   Suitable cases for amendment

13.2.1   If the error is in the surname of the deceased, the Registrar may order the grant to be revoked unless the amendment is of a minor nature.

13.2.2   If the forenames are shown incorrectly an amendment is normally allowed unless the sole forename is incorrect, in which case the grant will usually be revoked, unless the error is of a minor nature.

13.2.3   If an alias is required to be added to the grant, this can be done by way of amendment.

13.2.4   If the grant has not issued in the true name, it will be revoked and a further grant issued in the correct name.

13.2.5   The address of the deceased and the applicant, the date of death and any limitation can be amended.

13.2.6   An amendment to the name of the applicant is treated in the same manner as set out in sections 13.2.1 to 13.2.3 above.

13.2.7   An amendment to a grant to exclude or to include settled land can be made, provided that in the case of the latter the grant was not limited "save and except settled land". The Registrar may require evidence confirming that the value of the settled land was or was not included in the original grant.

13.3   Application for amendment of grant – procedure

13.3.1   The Registrar is empowered to amend the grant if he is satisfied that the amendment should be made.
(r. 41(1))

13.3.2   Section 13.3.1 above is subject to the consent of the grantee, unless there are circumstances which require the Registrar to make the order without such consent.
(r. 41(2))

13.3.3   It should be noted that the power to order amendment without the consent of the grantee will only be exercised in exceptional circumstances.
(r. 41(2))

13.3.4   The application to amend should be supported by an affidavit of facts setting out the grounds of the application and exhibiting any supporting documents (such as the death certificate if the error is in the date of death).

13.3.5   The application to amend should be made to the District Probate Registrar of the Registry from which the grant issued, or to the Record Keeper if the grant issued from the Principal Registry.

13.3.6   If the Registrar agrees to make the order, the grant is amended in red and a notation of the order made thereon.
          A precedent for the affidavit is given after paragraph 14.14 of the *Probate Manual*, 23rd edition.

Notation of grants

13.4

13.4.1   Certain subsequent actions which may affect the grant or the administrators are usually noted on the grant by the court.

13.4.2   Examples of section 13.4.1 above include:
          (a) orders under the Inheritance (Provision for Family and Dependents) Act 1975
          (b) the domicile of the deceased, if not shown on the grant when issued
          (c) retraction of renunciation (see section 15.8 below)
          (d) election to redeem a life interest
          (e) orders under s. 20(1) of the Administration of Justice Act 1982 for rectification of the will after the issue of the grant
          (f) addition of a further personal representative under s. 114(4) of the Supreme Court Act 1981.

13.4.3   In all cases in section 13.4.2 above, the notation is made on the original grant, which should be lodged for this purpose. Any copy of the grant issued subsequently will bear the notation.

13.4.4   Applications under section 13.4.2(b), (c) and (f) above are made ex-parte to the Registrar, supported by an affidavit of facts setting out the grounds of application.

13.4.5   It should be noted that an application under section 13.4.2(f) above can only be made if a life or minority interest arises. It cannot be used to add an administrator on any other grounds.

13.4.6   A spouse who elects to redeem a life interest (s. 47A of the Administration of Estates Act 1925) should within twelve months of the date of issue of the grant give notice of the election to the Senior Registrar by filing the appropriate notice (form 6 of the Rules) at the Principal Registry or at the district probate registry from which the grant issued.
(r. 56(1))

13.4.7   The notice referred to in section 13.4.6 above should be filed in duplicate if the grant issued from a district probate registry.
(r. 56(2))

REVOCATION OF GRANT

13.5   Introduction

13.5.1   On occasion it is necessary to revoke grants of representation and application has to be made to the High Court in order to effect this (Supreme Court Act 1981, s. 25(1)(b)).

13.5.2   Although an application is usually required, the court has the power to revoke a grant of its own motion if the matter requires such an exceptional course of action (Supreme Court Act 1981, s. 121(1)).

13.5.3   A revocation of a resealed grant is called a "cancellation" and is subject to the same terms as section 13.5.2 above (Supreme Court Act 1981, s. 121(3)).

13.6   Grounds for revocation or cancellation

13.6.1   The following are the most usual grounds for revocation or cancellation:
(a) a grant of letters of administration was obtained, when the deceased left a valid will;
(b) probate or letters of administration (with will) have been granted and a later, valid will is discovered;
(c) a codicil is found which affects the appointment of executors in the will;
(d) evidence is produced to show that the will admitted to proof is not valid;
(e) the grantee (or any of them) has died before the grant has issued;
(f) one of two or more executors has become incapable by reason of mental incapacity of managing his affairs (see section 13.8.1 below);

(g) one of two or more administrators has become incapable in the circumstances of (f) above;

(h) the grant has issued in respect of a living person.

13.6.2　If the sole executor or administrator has become incapable by reason of mental incapacity of managing his affairs, the grant is not revoked. A further grant may issue for the use and benefit of the incapable person.

13.6.3　The grant in section 13.6.2 above will be of administration *de bonis non* limited during the incapacity of the original grantee, unless the new grant is to issue to an executor who had power reserved, in which case the grant will be of double probate.

13.7　Procedure to obtain revocation

13.7.1　The application to revoke the grant (if not opposed) should be made to a Registrar, supported by an affidavit of facts and exhibiting the consent of the grantee if the application is not made by him.

13.7.2　The original grant or resealed Colonial grant should be lodged with the application but the revocation can still be made if the original documents are not available (Supreme Court Act 1981, s. 121(2) and (4)).

13.7.3　The application to revoke the grant should be made at the registry from which the original grant issued. If the grant issued from the Principal Registry, the affidavit and grant should be lodged with the Record Keeper.

13.7.4　If the grant has to be revoked on the grounds that a will or a later will has been discovered, the original will should be lodged for perusal by the Registrar.

13.8　Miscellaneous points

13.8.1　In the case of a revocation under section 13.6.1(f) only, a combined application for revocation and the new grant can be made.

13.8.2　The application under section 13.8.1 above may take the form of a combined affidavit of facts and an oath. The will need not be re-marked by the applicant in accordance with r. 10 and no Inland Revenue account is required, regardless of whether the estate is an excepted estate or not.

13.8.3   In every case save section 13.8.1 above, the grant must be revoked before the application for the new grant is made.

13.8.4   The oath to lead to the new grant should contain details of the old grant and of the order revoking it.
          See the precedents following paragraph 14.23 in the *Probate Manual*, 23rd edition.

13.8.5   A copy of the revoked grant, bearing the appropriate notation, should be lodged with the application for the new grant if this is being made at the Principal Registry. This is not necessary if application is made at a district probate registry.

13.8.6   The fee for the second grant is £2.

13.8.7   If an Inland Revenue account is required, the appropriate form should be lodged (see section 6.4 above).

DUPLICATE GRANTS

13.9   Introduction

13.9.1   A duplicate grant can be issued on the application of the grantee or of the extracting solicitor.

13.9.2   The grant issued will have the same date as the original and bear any notation carried by the original but will show the date the duplicate issued (on the right hand margin) and will have the words "Duplicate Grant" at the top.

13.9.3   The duplicate grant will be in the same form as the original but no copies will be issued and no record kept of its issue.

13.10   Procedure on application for a duplicate grant

13.10.1   Application for the duplicate should be made at the registry from which the original grant was issued. If the registry has closed since the issue of the grant, application should be made at the registry at which the records of the closed registry are kept.

13.10.2   When the application is made at the Principal Registry, a copy of the grant should be lodged. This is not necessary when application is made at a district probate registry.

13.10.3 If the original grant was obtained before 1 January 1934 (or 1 May 1934 in respect of a district probate registry grant), a certificate from the Capital Taxes Offices as to the amount of estate duty paid should be lodged with the application for the grant.

13.10.4 When the original grant was obtained at the Principal Registry before 1 January 1931, an engrossment of the testamentary documents may be required to be lodged.

13.10.5 Section 13.10.4 above applies to grants issued by the district probate registries before the photographic process was used to reproduce the wills.

13.10.6 The fee for a duplicate grant is £2.00.

14. Applications to the Court and Citations

Contents

EX-PARTE APPLICATIONS TO THE COURT

14.1 Introduction

14.1.1 Ex-parte applications should be made at the registry at which it is desired to make the application for the grant or from which the grant has issued.

14.1.2 The affidavit and supporting documents should be lodged with the Registrar of the district probate registry or with the probate department at the Principal Registry.

14.2   Orders which can be obtained by ex-parte application

14.2.1   Orders which can be obtained by way of ex-parte application include the following:

(a) an order under s. 114(2) of the Supreme Court Act 1981 permitting a grant to issue to a single administrator notwithstanding the existence of a life or minority interest;

(b) orders under r. 30 (see Chapter 7);

(c) an order for the assignment of guardians under r. 32 (see Chapter 8, sections 8.1 to 8.5);

(d) an order for a grant for the use and benefit of an incapable person (see Chapter 8, sections 8.6 to 8.9);

(e) an order to omit words of an offensive, libellous or blasphemous nature from a will;

(f) an order for rectification of the will under s. 20 of the Administration of Justice Act 1982 (provided that the application is unopposed);

(g) an order for leave to prove a copy, reconstructed or nuncupative will under r. 54;

(h) an order under r. 25(2) to join someone with no title to a grant with a person entitled under the Rules;

(i) an order under s. 116 of the Supreme Court Act 1981 (see Chapter 10, sections 10.13 to 10.14);

(j) an order under s. 113 of the Supreme Court Act 1981 (see Chapter 10, sections 10.10 to 10.12);

(k) an order for a grant of administration *ad colligenda bona* (see Chapter 10, sections 10.15 to 10.16);

(l) an order to appoint an additional administrator under s. 114(4) of the Supreme Court Act 1981 (see Chapter 13, sections 13.4.4 to 13.4.5);

(m) an order for the domicile of the deceased to be added to the grant;

(n) an order giving leave to retract a renunciation (see Chapter 16, section 16.8);

(o) an order to amend or revoke a grant (see Chapter 13, sections 13.1 to 13.8);

(p) an order giving leave to swear death (see Chapter 11, sections 11.5 to 11.7).

4.3   Summonses

4.3.1   If it is necessary to issue a summons in an application, it should be issued in the registry at which it is to be heard.

14.3.2   Most Registrars' summonses can be issued out of a district probate registry.

14.3.3   Summonses which can only be heard by a Family Division Registrar at the Principal Registry are:
         (a) an application under r. 44(13) in respect of an existing caveat after an appearance has been entered;
         (b) for an order under r. 45(3) regarding the issuing of a grant after the commencement of a probate action;
         (c) for an order under r. 46(3) in respect of a caveat in force at the commencement of citation proceedings.

14.4   Procedure in respect of a summons

14.4.1   The summons should be lodged in duplicate at the registry at which it is to be issued.

14.4.2   The summons should set out clearly the nature of the application and should contain the name and address of the issuing solicitor.

14.4.3   The registry will fix a hearing date and time and insert it on both copies of the summons. One copy will be retained by the registry and the other will be sealed with the seal of the court and returned to the solicitors.

14.4.4   A copy of the summons should be served personally or by registered post, recorded post or pre-paid post or by the Document Exchange. (r. 67)

14.4.5   Service of the summons should be effected upon those persons named therein.

14.4.6   A copy of any affidavit in support of the summons should be served with the summons.

14.4.7   The summons should be served at least two clear days before the hearing unless the Judge or Registrar at or before the hearing dispenses with service thereof. (r. 66(2))

14.4.8   If on the date appointed for the hearing any party to the summons does not attend, the Judge or Registrar may proceed and make such order as he thinks fit. Proof of service of the summons will be required in these circumstances.

14.4.9　If the parties to a summons agree and request an order in its terms, their consent should be added to the summons and the Registrar will be able to deal with it in their absence, subject to his discretion to call for the attendance of the parties if he thinks fit.

14.4.10　The order made on the summons will be drawn up and served by the registry at which it was made.

14.4.11　If any party wishes to appeal against the order made by the Registrar, he should do so by way of summons to a judge. (r. 65(1))

14.4.12　If any person other than the applicant appeared before the Registrar, a copy of the summons should be served upon him and the summons issued within seven days of the date of the order. (r. 65(2))

14.5　Order or subpoena to bring in the will

14.5.1　If a person who has a testamentary document in his possession, custody or power refuses to pass it to the executor or a person entitled to a grant, prove it or otherwise obstructs an application in respect thereof, he can be compelled to bring it into a district probate registry or the Principal Registry.

14.5.2　The Registrar may make an order requiring the person who has (or is believed to have) the testamentary document in his possession to attend before the court and be examined as to the document (Supreme Court Act 1981 s. 122(1)).

14.5.3　Once the person so ordered in section 14.5.2 above has attended before the court, he can be required to answer any questions in connection with the document and, if appropriate, he can be ordered to bring in the document in such manner as the court may direct (Supreme Court Act 1981 s. 122(2)).

14.5.4　Failure to comply with the order to attend, to answer questions in respect of the will or to lodge the will as directed may result in the committal to prison of the person so failing (Supreme Court Act 1981 s. 122(3)).

4.5.5　In order to bring into effect section 14.5.4 above, the order should be served personally with the appropriate penal notice endorsed thereon.

14.5.6   An alternative to the procedure in sections 14.5.2 to 14.5.5 above is for the applicant to make an application for the Registrar to issue a subpoena requiring the person suspected of having the testamentary document in his possession, custody or power to lodge it at the appropriate district probate registry or at the Principal Registry (Supreme Court Act 1981 s. 123).

14.5.7   The application to issue the subpoena should be made by lodging two copies of the subpoena and an affidavit in support at any district probate registry or at the Principal Registry.

14.5.8   If required, a draft subpoena and affidavit can be settled by the Registrar of the registry at which the application is to be made. A fee of £5 is charged for settling each document.

14.5.9   The registry at which the will is to be lodged (usually the registry from which the subpoena issued) must be specified in the subpoena.

14.5.10 Once the sealed copy of the subpoena has been returned by the registry, it should be endorsed with a penal notice and served personally with a copy of the affidavit in support.
(r. 50(2))

14.5.11 Enforcement of the subpoena may be effected by committal.

14.5.12 If the testamentary document is in the possession of the person to whom the subpoena is directed, he should lodge it as directed in the subpoena.

14.5.13 If the testamentary document is not in the possession of the person named in the subpoena, he may file an affidavit stating this in the registry from which the subpoena issued.
(r. 50(2))

CITATIONS

14.6   Introduction

14.6.1   If a person with an interest in the estate wishes to compel the other persons with an interest therein either to make the application for grant or to lose their right to apply, a citation may be issued.

14.6.2 The contents of the citation must be verified by an affidavit sworn by the citor, save that in special circumstances an affidavit sworn by the citor's solicitor may be accepted.
(r. 46(2))

14.6.3 The citor should enter a caveat before the issue of the citation.
(r. 46(3))

14.6.4 The citation should be served personally, unless the Registrar directs otherwise. It is open to the Registrar to order that service of the citation be effected by advertisement.
(r. 46(4))

14.6.5 Every will which is referred to in a citation should be lodged at the Registry from which it is to be issued before the citation is issued.
(r. 44(5))

14.6.6 The Registrar has the jurisdiction to allow the citation to issue without the original will being lodged if it is not in the citor's possession and the Registrar is satisfied that it is not practical for it to be lodged.
(r. 44(5))

14.6.7 A citation may issue from any district probate registry or from the Principal Registry.
(r. 46(1))

14.6.8 Every citation must be settled by the Registrar of the registry from which it is to issue.
(r. 46(1))

14.6.9 In practice, section 14.6.8 above is extended to the extent that a draft of the affidavit in support should be lodged with the draft citation to enable the Registrar to comment as to any appropriate amendments, when the latter is lodged to be settled.

14.6.10 If the Registrar orders service of the citation by advertisement as in section 14.6.4 above, a draft advertisement must be lodged, together with a sealed copy of the citation, at the registry from which it issued. The Registrar will settle the advertisement and direct in which newspapers or other publications the advertisement is to be placed and the number of times it is to appear.

14.6.11 A fee of £5 each is payable for settling the draft citation and advertisement. No fee is charged for perusing and commenting on the draft affidavit. The drafts must be lodged when the engrossed and sworn documents are lodged for issue.

14.7   Citation to accept or refuse a grant

14.7.1   If the person with the prior title to the grant refuses to extract the grant or to renounce, it is open to anyone with a lower title to issue a citation directed to the person with the prior title to accept or refuse the grant.
(r. 47(1))

14.7.2   A citation may be issued in respect of an executor to whom power has been reserved by any of the executors who have proved the will or the executors of the last surviving of the deceased proving executors.
(r. 47(2))

14.7.3   The citation may be directed to more than one person.

14.7.4   Care should be taken to ascertain that all persons with a prior title to the citor have been cited to accept or refuse the grant.

14.7.5   Difficulties may arise in respect of a citation directed to a corporate body. It must be established whether the company in question is or is not a trust corporation and the citation worded accordingly.

14.7.6   A creditor may issue a citation in case of a whole or partial intestacy and if the deceased died without any known kin, the citation should state that fact and notice of the application should be given to the Treasury Solicitor by sending him a copy of the citation.
(r. 38)

14.7.7   The citation should contain the full name and address of the citor, the deceased and the person or persons cited. The entitlement to the grant of the citor and the person cited should be set out and any necessary clearing included.

14.7.8   The citation should direct that any appearance be entered at the registry from which the citation issued within eight days of service of the citation and put the persons cited on notice that in the absence of an appearance being entered, the court will grant administration to the citor.

14.7.9   The citation should be dated and state the name and address of the citor or, if he is acting through solicitors, the name and address of the extracting solicitors. It will be sealed with the seal of the court and signed by the Registrar.

14.8 Citation to take a grant of probate

14.8.1 If an executor has intermeddled in the estate, he is not permitted to renounce probate. (For further details on intermeddling and renunciation, see Chapter 16, sections 16.3.3 to 16.3.5.)

14.8.2 An intermeddling executor may be compelled to take a grant of probate by way of a citation.
(r. 47(3))

14.8.3 The citation may be issued by any person who has an interest in the estate, after the expiration of six months from the date of death of the deceased.
(r. 47(3))

14.8.4 It should be noted that no such citation can be issued if proceedings in respect of the validity of the will are pending.
(r. 47(3))

14.8.5 The form of the citation is as set out in sections 14.7.7 to 14.7.9 above.

14.8.6 The citation should request the intermeddling executor to show cause why he should not take a grant of probate.

14.8.7 The affidavit in support of the citation should also set out the acts of intermeddling.

14.9 Citation to propound a testamentary document

14.9.1 A citation to propound a will may be issued by a person with an interest under an earlier will or an intestacy.
(r. 48(1))

14.9.2 The citation should be directed to the executor of the will and to all persons who have an interest under the will.
(r. 48(1))

14.9.3 The citation should be in the same general form as set out in sections 14.7.7 and 14.7.9 above.

14.9.4 The citation should direct the appearance as in section 14.7.8 above and should direct those persons named therein to propound the will (the term "propound" means that application should be made to have the purported testamentary document pronounced for in solemn form in the Chancery Division).

14.9.5 In default of the person cited propounding the testamentary document, the citation should request that the application for the grant proceed as though the testamentary document were invalid.

14.10 Appearance to citation

14.10.1 An appearance to the citation should be entered in form 5 of the Rules at the registry from which it issued.
(r. 46(6))

14.10.2 A sealed copy of the appearance should be served forthwith upon the citor by the person entering the appearance.
(r. 46(6))

14.10.3 The appearance should contain the caveat number and date of entry, the date of the citation, the full name and address of the deceased and of the citor, the citor's interest in the estate and the full name and address and the interest of the person entering the appearance. The citee must have an address for service in England and Wales.

14.10.4 The appearance should be entered within eight days of the service of the citation or at any time if no application in respect of the citation has been made by the citor.
(r. 46(6))

14.11 Procedure subsequent to an appearance – citation to accept or refuse a grant

14.11.1 When the person cited has entered an appearance, he should apply ex-parte by affidavit to the Registrar for an order that a grant should issue to himself.
(r. 47(4))

14.11.2 If the person cited has entered an appearance but has not applied for an order as in section 14.11.1 above, or has not proceeded with his application for a grant (after obtaining such order) with reasonable diligence, the citor may apply to a Registrar by way of a summons for an order that a grant issues to himself.
(r. 47(7)(a))

14.11.3 When the citation has issued in respect of an executor to whom power has been reserved and the circumstances in section 14.11.2 above apply, the citor may issue a summons to the Registrar for an order striking out the appearance and making an endorsement on the grant to the effect that the executor in respect of whom power has been reserved has been duly cited, has not appeared and that all his rights in respect of the executorship have wholly ceased.
(r. 47(7)(b))

14.12   Procedure subsequent to an appearance – citation to take a grant

14.12.1 When the person cited has entered an appearance he should apply ex-parte by affidavit to the Registrar for an order that a grant issue to himself.
(r. 47(4))

14.12.2 In the circumstances of section 14.11.2 above, the citor may apply by way of summons to the Registrar for an order requiring the person cited to take out the grant within a specified time or for a grant to issue to himself or to some other person nominated for this purpose in the summons.
(r. 47(7)(c))

14.13   Procedure subsequent to an appearance – citation to propound

14.13.1 If the person cited to propound the will enters an appearance, he should commence an action in the Chancery Division by way of a writ, or in the County Court if appropriate, depending upon the value of the estate.

14.13.2 If an appearance has been entered but the person cited takes no action, the citor may issue a summons before the Registrar for an order that a grant of representation may issue as if the will was invalid.
(r. 48(2)(b))

14.13.3 The application in section 14.13.2 above should be supported by an affidavit proving that service of the summons has been effected.

14.14   Citation to accept or refuse a grant – no appearance entered

14.14.1 If the person cited has not entered an appearance to the citation, the citor may apply to the Registrar for an order that the grant may issue to himself.
(r. 47(5)(a))

14.14.2 If the citation was in respect of an executor to whom power has been reserved, application should be made to the Registrar for an order that an endorsement be made on the grant that the executor to whom power has been reserved has been cited and has not appeared and that all his entitlement as executor has wholly ceased. (r. 47(5)(b))

14.14.3 An affidavit in support of the application in sections 14.14.1 or 2 above should be supported by an affidavit proving that service of the citation has been effected.
(r. 47(6))

14.15   Citation to take a grant – no appearance entered

14.15.1 If no appearance has been entered by the person cited, the citor should issue a summons to the Registrar (which should be served upon the person cited) for an order that the person cited should take a grant within a specified period or that the grant may issue to himself or to some other person specified in the summons.
(r. 47(5)(c))

14.15.2 The summons in section 14.15.1 above should be supported by an affidavit proving that service of the citation has been effected.
(r. 47(6))

14.16   Citation to propound a will – no appearance entered

14.16.1 If no appearance has been entered to the citation, application may be made to the Registrar for an order that a grant may issue as if the will were invalid.
(r. 48(2)(a))

14.16.2 The application in section 14.16.1 above should be supported by an affidavit proving that service of the citation upon the person cited has been effected.
(r. 48(2)(a))
    For precedents for the form of citation and affidavit, see those following paragraph 15.30 of the *Probate Manual*, 23rd edition.

4.17 Citations – miscellaneous points

4.17.1 A citation can be served upon a person under a disability.

4.17.2 Service upon a minor can be effected by serving the papers upon his father or guardian. In default of there being either, service may be effected upon the person with whom the minor is residing or in whose care he is at the time (O. 80, Rules of the Supreme Court 1965).

4.17.3 In the case of a person who is a patient, service of the citation is effected upon the person authorised by the Court of Protection. If there is no such person, service should be effected upon the person in whose care he is or with whom he resides.

4.17.4 If the person under a disability does not have an appearance entered on his behalf, an application should be made to the Registrar to consider whether a guardian should be assigned to the person under the disability for this purpose (O. 80, r. 6 Rules of the Supreme Court 1965).

4.17.5 The fee for settling a citation is £5.00.

15. Standing Searches and Caveats

STANDING SEARCHES

15.1

15.1.1   If it is required to be notified of the issue of a grant, notice in form 2 of the Rules should be lodged with the Senior Registrar. (r. 43(1))

15.1.2   The form should contain the full name and address of the deceased, any alias names and the exact date of death.

15.1.3   An office copy of any grant issued in the estate of a person in which a standing search has been entered, provided that it has not issued more than twelve months before the entry of a standing search *or* that it issues within six months after the entry of the standing search, will be sent to the person entering the standing search. (r. 43(2))

15.1.4   A standing search can be extended at the end of the six month period by making application at the Principal Registry. (r. 43(3)(a))

15.1.5   An extension of the standing search as set out in section 15.1.4 above should be applied for in the last month of the period of six months and will be effective for a further period of six months. (r. 43(3)(b))

15.1.6 The standing search can be extended as in sections 15.1.4 and 15.1.5 above any number of times.
(r. 43(3)(c))

15.1.7 The application for the entry of a standing search should be made to the Record Keeper, Principal Registry of the Family Division, Somerset House, Strand, London WC2R 1LP.

15.1.8 The fee for entering or extending a standing search is £2.00.

CAVEATS

15.2   Introduction

15.2.1 If any person wishes to ensure that no grant of representation is sealed or resealed without notice to him, he may enter a caveat.
(r. 44(1))

15.2.2 The caveat may be entered at any district probate registry or sub-registry or at the Principal Registry.
(r. 44(1))

15.2.3 A caveat prevents the issue of any grant (except a grant *ad colligenda bona* or under s. 117 of the Supreme Court Act 1981) to anyone save the person who entered the caveat.

15.2.4 A caveat entered on the day upon which the grant is sealed or resealed will not prevent its issue.
(r. 44(1))

15.3   Caveats – form and procedure

15.3.1 A caveat can be entered either by a party in person or by a solicitor acting on his behalf.

15.3.2 The caveat should be in form 3 of the Rules and be entered either:
(a) by completing the form in the appropriate book at any registry or sub-registry, or
(b) by sending through the post a notice in form 3 (at the caveator's own risk) to any registry or sub-registry.
(r. 44(2))

15.3.3   The caveat should contain the full name and last address of the deceased, the date of death of the deceased and the full name of the caveator. It should be dated and signed by the caveator if he is acting in person or by the solicitor acting on his behalf.
(form 3)

15.3.4   The caveat must contain an address for service on the caveator in England and Wales.
(r. 49)

15.3.5   Upon entry, an acknowledgement will be issued by the registry in which the caveat has been entered.

15.3.6   A caveat will expire six months after its entry.
(r. 44(3)(a))

15.3.7   The caveator may extend the caveat provided this is done within the last month before its expiry by either attending in person or by writing to the registry at which the caveat was entered. A caveat can be extended any number of times in the same manner, subject to sections 15.3.8 and 15.3.9 below.
(r. 44(3))

15.3.8   A caveat will not expire as in section 15.3.6 above if:
(a) an appearance to a warning has been entered (r. 44(13)); or
(b) the caveat was in force at the commencement of citation proceedings (r. 46(3)); or
(c) a summons for directions under r. 44(6) is pending (r. 44(8)).

15.3.9   The commencement of a probate action prevents the issue of a grant until application is made by the person entitled to apply under the terms of the order made at the conclusion of the action.
(r. 45(3))

15.3.10 A caveat may be withdrawn by the caveator at any time, unless an appearance to a warning has been entered (r. 44(11)). If a summons under r. 44(6) has been issued, the Registrar may have to give directions.

15.3.11 A withdrawal of a caveat must be made at the registry or sub-registry at which it was entered, either by attending there or by post. The receipt of entry (see section 15.3.5 above) should be produced.
(r. 44(11))

15.3.12 It should be noted that if a caveat has been warned, the caveator should give notice to the person warning of the withdrawal of the caveat.

15.4   Warnings

15.4.1   If any person with an interest in the estate wishes to put the caveator on notice that he should enter an appearance stating his contrary interest, he should enter a warning in form 4 of the Rules.
(r. 44(5))

15.4.2   The warning must be entered at the registry in which the index of caveats is kept.
(r. 44(5))

15.4.3   The warning may be entered by personal attendance at the registry in which is maintained the caveat index or by post.

15.4.4   The warning should state the interest in the estate of the person warning and should require the caveator to state his interest in the estate contrary to that of the person warning or, if he has no such contrary interest, to issue a summons under r. 44(6), within eight days of service of the warning upon him.
(r. 44(5))

15.4.5   Service of the warning should be effected forthwith upon the caveator by the person warning, either personally or by leaving it at the address for service of the caveator given on the caveat, or by sending it by pre-paid post or by DX to that address.

15.5   Appearance to the warning

15.5.1   The caveator may within the eight day period specified in the warning (or at any time up to the filing of an affidavit in accordance with section 15.8 below) enter an appearance thereto in form 5 of the Rules setting out his interest in the estate contrary to that of the person warning.
(r. 44(10))

15.5.2   The appearance must be entered by way of personal attendance at the registry in which the index of caveats is kept.
(r. 44(10))

15.5.3   A sealed copy of the appearance should be served forthwith by the caveator upon the person warning it by leaving it or sending it by pre-paid, recorded or registered post or by the Document Exchange to him at the address given for service on the warning.
(r. 44(10))

15.6 Summons for directions

15.6.1 If the caveator does not have an interest contrary to that of the person warning, he may issue a summons for directions. The summons should indicate what direction will be sought at the hearing.

15.6.2 The summons should be issued within the time for entry of an appearance (r. 44(6)). See section 15.5.1 above.

15.6.3 The summons is heard by a Registrar.

15.6.4 At the hearing of the summons, the Registrar may make any direction he thinks appropriate, including a direction that the caveat should cease to have effect.
(r. 44(7))

15.6.5 Unless the Registrar directs otherwise (or the caveat is withdrawn), the caveat remains in force in the event that a summons under this rule is issued until the summons is finally disposed of, notwithstanding that more than six months may elapse before this takes place.
(r. 44(8))

15.7 Subsequent procedure to an appearance

15.7.1 If an appearance is entered, the next stage in the proceedings is usually for the person warning to commence proceedings in the Chancery Division or the County Court if appropriate.

15.7.2 If the parties come to an agreement before the Chancery Division (or County Court) proceedings are commenced in respect of the matter, a consent summons may be issued in the Principal Registry for consideration by a Family Division Registrar.

15.7.3 The summons in section 15.7.2 above should request the removal of the caveat upon the grant issuing to the person entitled under the Rules.

15.7.4 The consent to the order should be endorsed on the summons by the parties acting in person or by their solicitors if they are legally represented.

5.8   Non-appearance to warning

5.8.1   If the caveator does not enter an appearance to the warning or issue a summons in accordance with section 15.6 above, the person warning may file an affidavit as to service of the warning if he wishes to have the caveat removed.
(r. 44(12))

5.8.2   The affidavit must be filed at the registry at which the caveat index is held.
(r. 44(12))

5.8.3   If a search of the relevant records at the registry at which the caveat index is held reveals that no appearance has been entered and that no summons under r. 44(6) is pending, the caveat is removed.

5.8.4   It should be noted that if the caveator wishes to enter a further caveat when the previous one has been removed in accordance with this section, he must first obtain leave of a Registrar at the Principal Registry.
(r. 44(14))

5.9   Miscellaneous points

5.9.1   A caveat does not prevent the issue of the grant to a person other than the caveator if the caveator is one of the applicants.

5.9.2   It should be noted that in the event of a dispute between two parties of equal title, the correct procedure is to issue a summons under r. 27(6).
See sections 14.3 to 14.4 above for further details.

16. Renunciation and Retraction

Contents

RENUNCIATION

16.1 Introduction

16.1.1 It is open to a person entitled to a grant of representation to renounc
his right to the grant if he wishes.

16.1.2 A renunciation must be expressed in terms which are final an
without qualification

16.1.3 A renunciation operates from the date it is signed but is not bindin
until it is filed, this being defined as the date the grant issues.

16.1.4 It follows from section 16.1.3 above that a renunciation may b
withdrawn at any time up to the issue of the grant.

16.2 Renunciation – form

16.2.1 A renunciation should be in the form suitable to the type (
application.
See the precedents following paragraph 17.12 of the *Proba*
Manual, 23rd edition.

16.2.2 The renunciation may be executed by more than one person provide
that their full name and entitlements to the grant are shown.

.2.3   The act of renunciation should be witnessed by a disinterested person and dated.

.2.4   A renunciation by a company may be under seal but in cases in which this is not done, a certified copy of the resolution identifying those persons entitled to renounce on behalf of the company should be lodged with the renunciation.

.3   Renunciation of executorship

.3.1   An executor who wishes to renounce probate should execute the appropriate form in accordance with section 16.2 above.

.3.2   A renunciation of probate does not affect the renunciant's title to a grant of administration (with will) if he is entitled in this capacity. (r. 37(1))

.3.3   An executor who has intermeddled in an estate cannot renounce probate.

.3.4   "Intermeddling" may be defined as the action of an executor commencing to undertake the duties of executorship.

.3.5   It has been held that a trivial act of intermeddling may not preclude renunciation (*Holder v Holder* [1968] Ch 338).

.3.6   If an executor swears the papers to lead to a grant of probate and then wishes to renounce, he may do so provided that he has not undertaken any duties as executor other than those of a trivial nature.

.3.7   A renunciation of probate must contain the statement that the executor has not intermeddled in the estate and will not intermeddle therein with the intent to defraud creditors.

.4   Renunciation of letters of administration (with will)

.4.1   The exact title of the renunciant to the grant must be stated in the renunciation.

.4.2   It should be noted that in the event of a person being entitled to a grant both as an executor and as a trustee or beneficiary in the estate, he should renounce his right to a grant in both capacities if he has a prior title to that of the applicant.

16.5   Renunciation of letters of administration

16.5.1   A renunciation of letters of administration follows the same basi
         principles as the previous renunciations and should set out the exac
         title of the renunciant.

16.5.2   A renunciation of letters of administration will not allow a grant t
         issue to someone who is not entitled to a grant in accordance with th
         order of priority as set out in r. 22.

16.6   Other renunciations

16.6.1   It is possible for a person entitled to a grant to appoint an attorney t
         renounce on his behalf, provided that the authority to do so i
         specifically included in the renunciation (*Re Rosser's Goods* (1864
         Sw & Tr 490).

16.6.2   A guardian specifically assigned by Registrar's order for the purpos
         can renounce a minor's right to a grant of letters of administratio
         (with or without will).
         (r. 34(2))

16.6.3   It is not possible for anyone to renounce a minor executor's right t
         grant of probate on his behalf.
         (r. 34(1))

16.6.4   The Court of Protection may authorise by way of an order the perso
         named in that order to renounce the right to a grant of representatio
         on behalf of a person who is by reason of mental incapacity incapabl
         of managing his affairs.

16.7   Renunciations – miscellaneous

16.7.1   A renunciation is usually filed when the application for the grant i
         made but an executor to whom power has been reserved should fil
         his renunciation after the grant issues.

16.7.2   It is open to the person entitled to a grant under the terms of a will t
         renounce his rights thereto upon the death of the testator and befor
         the application for the grant. In these circumstances, the renun
         ciation and will may be filed in any district probate registry or wit
         the Record Keeper at the Principal Registry. The renunciation i
         examined upon lodgment and if it is found to be incorrect (e.g. i
         does not set out all the capacities of the renunciant in which h
         desires to renounce), it will be rejected.

16.7.3 Once the renunciation, will and any codicils have been filed as set out in section 16.7.2 above, they are retained in that registry and not released other than to another registry. It therefore follows that when the application is made, the applicants will have to attend at the registry in which the will is filed (or at another more convenient registry to which the will has been sent) to swear the papers and mark the will unless the Registrar permits a copy of the will to be marked under r. 10 (2).

16.7.4 If a renunciation is executed in a non-English-speaking country and is in the English language, it should be executed before a notary or a British consular official.

16.7.5 In the event that section 16.7.4 above applies and the renunciation is not executed before the persons mentioned above, evidence that the renunciant understands English will have to be filed.

16.7.6 If the renunciation is not in English, a suitable translation should be filed.

16.7.7 It should be noted that a renunciation filed in a foreign court in respect of proceedings in that court is not effective in England and Wales and if the renunciant wishes to renounce in England and Wales he should file a further renunciation.

16.7.8 A renunciation of administration in one capacity (e.g. as residuary legatee and devisee) debars the renunciant from taking a grant of administration in a lower capacity (e.g. as a legatee) unless the Registrar otherwise directs.
(r. 37(2)).

RETRACTION

16.8

16.8.1 Although a renunciation is regarded as being final once the grant has issued (see section 16.1. above), it is open to the renunciant to apply to the Registrar for leave to retract his renunciation.
(r. 37(3))

16.8.2 Leave will only be given so to do in the most exceptional circumstances in the case of an executor who has renounced probate and the grant issued to someone in a lower capacity.
(r. 37(3))

16.8.3   A person entitled to a grant of administration who wishes to retract his renunciation should show it is necessary that he should be granted leave so to do. This would arise, for example, in the case of an estate which had not been fully administered and a further administrator cannot be found.

16.8.4   The application for leave to retract is made ex-parte to the Registrar supported by an affidavit of facts and the original grant (or an office copy thereof).

16.8.5   The application to retract may be made at the registry at which the renunciation is filed or at the Principal Registry.
(r. 37(4))

16.8.6   If leave to retract is granted, the applicant should complete the form of retraction and lodge it when he makes application for the new grant.
        For the form of retraction, see that following paragraph 17.16 of the *Probate Manual*, 23rd edition.

17. Common Practice Errors

Contents

17.1 Introduction

17.1.1 Many applications cannot proceed by reason of avoidable technical errors which cause unnecessary delay and which, with the help of this chapter, may be avoided in the future.

17.1.2 A brief check of the papers before swearing, using the guidelines set out below, may bring to light those errors which cause the majority of cases to be delayed.

17.1.3 This chapter will be divided into errors in wills, oaths and practice.

17.2 Errors in wills

17.2.1 The position of the testator's signature may require evidence as to execution of the will.

17.2.2 The Wills Act 1837 (as amended) validates a will if signed by the testator with the intention to give effect to it.

17.2.3 Although there is no longer a requirement for the testator to sign "at the foot or end thereof", evidence may well be required if the signature is in any other place (see sections 2.1.2 to 2.1.3 above).

17.2.4 If the testator signs the will in the attestation clause, affidavit evidence as to execution will be required unless the provisions of r. 12(3) apply.

17.2.5   Where evidence is required when section 17.2.4 above applies, this is because the attestation clause is a statement made by the witnesses and is therefore not in the testator's part of the will. The name of the testator appearing therein may not necessarily have been in execution of the will.

17.2.6   The witnesses should sign below the testator's signature. Any variation on this may require evidence to show that execution was in accordance with the Wills Act 1837.

17.2.7   Wills with an appointment of executor which on the face of it is not valid are very often presented for proof without any attempt to establish the validity of the appointment, e.g. appointments with the wording "one of the partners", "A or B", "any two of A, B or C". Reference in such cases may be made to the registry at which it is desired to prove the will as to whether extrinsic evidence can be admitted to validate the appointment before the papers are sworn.

17.2.8   S. 21 of the Administration of Justice Act 1982, which applies where the deceased died on or after 1 January 1983, is especially useful if it is desired to try and establish the validity of an appointment as set out in section 17.2.7 above. In such applications, an affidavit should be filed setting out the facts of the case and what the testator's expressed intentions were. Any supporting documents should be exhibited.

17.2.9   The attestation clause is often incorrectly drawn.

17.2.10 To be valid, the attestation clause must show that the testator signed (or acknowledged his signature) in the presence of the witnesses, who then signed (or signed or acknowledged their signatures, if the testator died on or after 1 January 1983) in his presence. If either of these elements is missing, the Registrar will require evidence as to execution unless the provisions of r. 12(3) apply.

17.2.11 A printed signature by the testator (unless there is an explanation in the attestation clause) or from either of the witnesses may require evidence of execution and, in the former case, of the testator's knowledge of contents of the will.

17.2.12 Similarly, a mark made by the testator in execution of the will (unless a suitable attestation clause is provided) usually requires affidavit evidence from one of the witnesses confirming good execution and of the testator's knowledge of contents of the will.

17.2.13 Any unauthenticated alteration in the will (unless it is minor and of no significance) will require evidence to show whether it was made before or after execution to establish whether or not it may be proved as part of the will.

17.2.14 If the will is not dated anywhere, evidence as to the date is required and the application will not be able to proceed until the date has been confirmed by way of affidavit evidence.

17.2.15 If the possibility of incorporation arises (see section 2.2.4 above), the Registrar may be consulted before the papers are sworn. The question of incorporation must be decided before the papers are lodged, otherwise delay will occur whilst the case is stopped and the document examined. If it is decided that the document should be incorporated, further delays will be occasioned by having the papers resworn.

17.2.16 The marking of the will and codicils as required by r. 10 must be by way of the *signatures* of the applicant and the person before whom the oath is sworn. Failure to do this will result in the documents being returned by the registry to be properly marked.

17.3   *Checklist*

17.3.1   Section 17.3.2 below is a simple checklist of points to consider in respect of a will. It is not intended to be exhaustive but will cover most of the areas in which errors occur.

17.3.2   (a) Has the will been *signed* by the testator? If so, does the form or position of the signature indicate that the correct mode of execution has been followed?
(b) If there is any doubt, has evidence on this point been obtained?
(c) Is there any doubt over the appointment of executors?
(d) Does the will bear a *date* anywhere?
(e) Does the attestation clause indicate that the will has been *properly executed?*
(f) Does the *position of the witnesses' signatures* give rise to doubts that execution was in the correct form?
(g) Is there any question as to the *form of the witnesses' signature?* If so, evidence is most likely to be required.
(h) Are there any *unauthenticated alterations* in the will which require evidence to determine in which form the will is to be proved?
(i) Is there any working in the will which may serve to *incorporate some other document?*

(j) Have the will and codicils been properly *marked* in accordance with r. 10?

17.4   Errors in the oath

17.4.1   A final check of the name of the deceased and the applicants against those shown in the will quite often results in a discrepancy being found. Any differences in names should be accounted for in the oath. (See sections 3.2 and 4.9 above for further details.)

17.4.2   Has the applicant's full name been shown in the oath? A comparison of the signature of the applicant with the name on the oath will sometimes reveal an extra initial indicating a further forename which has not been included in the oath. This is often the case when the applicant appears to have only one forename. Such a check is common registry practice and results in a high number of errors being discovered.

17.4.3   The wording of the appointment of executors determines those persons entitled to apply for a grant (see sections 3.2.12 to 3.2.13 above).

17.4.4   Care should be taken to ensure that the correct applicants have been chosen. In the event that a firm has been appointed executor the fact that the applicants were partners at the date of death or at the date of the will (whichever is appropriate) must be sworn in the oath.

17.4.5   All such partners in the firm should be named in the oath and those not applying accounted for, either by way of renunciation or by stating that they have power reserved.

17.4.6   The fact that notice has been given under r. 27(1) to all executors to whom power has been reserved must be recited in the body of the oath and not in a side-note.

17.4.7   The clearing in a case of administration (with will) when the applicant's title is derived under r. 20(c) (see section 4.4 above) must be included in full. Failure to do so will result in the oath having to be resworn.

17.4.8   It is always worthwhile to check (before the oath is sworn) that everyone with a superior title to that of the applicant has been cleared off in the oath. If there is a break in the clearing, the oath will have to be resworn.

7.4.9   In all cases of administration (with or without will) the sections on life and minority interests must be completed. If either is omitted, the case cannot proceed until this point has been resolved.

7.4.10   When it is necessary in a case of administration to establish the title of the applicant by describing his relationship to the deceased, the word "lawful" is often omitted. This may not be necessary in certain circumstances (see section 5.13.3 above), but it is always necessary in the case of a surviving spouse. Any other form of wording (e.g. "the surviving spouse", "the widower/widow", "the husband/wife") will result in the oath having to be resworn.

7.4.11   Failure to include the appropriate limitation in the oath (e.g. on an application by an attorney "for the use and benefit of the said *A. B.* and until further representation be granted") will result in the case being delayed.

7.4.12   The gross and net figures or the 'band' figures if the estate is an "excepted estate" must be included in the oath. If the estate is an "excepted estate" (see section 6.3 above), the wording "and this is not a case in which an Inland Revenue account is required to be delivered" must appear in the oath. If it is omitted, the oath will have to be resworn.

7.5   *Checklist*

7.5.1   Section 17.5.2 below is a simple checklist of points to check in respect of the oath in general. As in section 17.3.2 above, it is not intended to be exhaustive.

7.5.2   (a) Do the *names* of the deceased and the applicant shown on the oath *agree* with those in the will? If not, have all the variations been accounted for?
          (b) Have the applicants signed the oath or Inland Revenue account with any *extra initials*, indicating an additional fore-name not disclosed in the will or on the oath?
          (c) If there is a *discrepancy* between the names of the applicants as shown on the oath and in the will, has this been accounted for in the oath?
          (d) Has the *domicile* been included?
          (e) Have the statements on *settled land, life and minority interests* all been completed?
          (f) Has the *full clearing* been included?
          (g) Has the applicant's *title* been set out in full?

(h) Has the relationship of the applicant to the deceased been described as "lawful" if this is required?

(i) Has the appropriate *limitation* been included?

(j) Have the *gross* and *net amounts* of the estate been included? If the estate is an "excepted estate", have the appropriate "band" figures been used (i.e. appropriate to those in force at the date of death)? In the case of an "excepted estate", have the words "and this is not a case in which an Inland Revenue account is required to be delivered" been included?

17.6   Miscellaneous practice points

17.6.1   Where the estate is not an "excepted estate" the correct form of Inland Revenue account must be used (see section 6.4 above). Failure to do so will result in delay.

17.6.2   The correct fee should be included with the application for the grant. Although an overpayment does not cause delay (notwithstanding the expense incurred by the registry in making the refund) delays can be occasioned by a request for further fees in the event of an underpayment. The current fees order is the Supreme Court (Non-Contentious Probate) Fees Order 1981 as amended.

17.6.3   Although this seems obvious, it is surprising how many applications are made without a vital document such as the will or oath being lodged. A brief check of the contents is always worthwhile.

17.6.4   Any previously settled documents should be lodged with the application.

17.6.5   It is of great assistance if any previous correspondence concerning the case is mentioned when application is made for the grant. Any reference should be quoted.